Making Se[...]
Incredible Li[...].

Thoughts of a Third Culture Kid Therapist

Dr Rachel Cason

Dear Nicole,
May you always
be aware of your
own courage.
Rachel

First published in the United Kingdom in 2023 by Life Story Therapies.

www.explorelifestory.com

Copyright ©2023 Dr Rachel Cason.

Layout and design by Darren Hendley. Set in Baskerville.
www.darrenhendley.co.uk

1 2 3 4 5 27 26 25 24 23

ISBN: 978-1-3999-5310-8

I dedicate this book to my darling girl. The way you fill the pages of your own story delights and inspires me. You love generously, challenge constantly and are relentlessly true to your own self. I love you.

Praise for Making Sense of Incredible Lives

"Incredible Lives and the Courage to Live Them" is an accessible book of short, conversational, topic-based chapters. This book represents a welcome change to one who did ATCK research in the 1990s. At that time most ATCKs had no term to frame this common cultural experience, so those who had repatriated to U.S. often felt alone and terminally weird. Those who had sought a therapist's help invariably reported "they just don't get it." Cason gets it. Not only has she actively listened to her clients' stories, but she has lived the life and can share her own story.

Cason reports widely recognized themes describing lives of long term, mobile TCKs, e.g.: change as a constant, needing to adapt and readapt, questions of identity and home, sense of loss on many fronts. She shows how elements of the TCK experience can make adult repatriation difficult for the ATCK and impossible for others to understand. ATCKs know they have led privileged lives, that they are adaptable and resilient , thus may feel any repatriation problems are their own fault.

Given their mobile, changing life histories, settling and commitment can be frightening for many who feel trapped, feel that without travel they are no longer interesting, and worry they are unable to contribute using their TCK skills. She understands and validates such feelings and fears. She normalizes them for this population; "it is not your fault". She provides helpful suggestions for how to move forward even if settled into an unfamiliar world by honoring and building on past experiences and strengths rather than denying or hiding them, and by learning to understand and appreciate yet another "new" culture.

This book will be familiar and comforting to repatriated ATCKs and a base of understanding for friends who have not shared such a childhood."

Dr. Ann Baker Cottrell, Professor Emerita, TCK researcher

In *Incredible Lives and the Courage to Lead Them* Cason brings together some of her keenest insights from years of writing, updated and revised into a beautiful book. The wide range of topics she covers include conversations many adult TCKs I talk to say they wish they were having in wider communities. This content is important, not only for adult TCKs but also for parents and caregivers. It reads like a novel, meandering from topic to topic, taking the reader on a journey even as it invites self-reflection and hope for one's own journey of identity and building a life of balance and peace.

Tanya Crossman, author of Misunderstood: The Impact of Growing Up Overseas in the 21st Century

"From trauma to relationships to identity to friendship to racism, Rachel Cason emerges as a gentle guide for the hearts and souls of third culture kids. As a professional and gifted therapist, she takes her work out of the office and onto the page, bringing up topics that are often pushed to the side instead of gently confronted. I cannot begin to describe how necessary and important this book is to the TCK world. We are in an era of massive mental health challenges and displacement, two things that are too familiar to many third culture kids. Depression, loneliness, and a struggle to belong are a living reality as third culture kids enter adulthood and long to make sense of their journeys. Rachel knows this but doesn't leave us hanging in a lonely, solitary, struggle. Instead, she asks us to explore our stories completely and fully, giving us permission, courage, and hope to live our incredible lives well."

Marilyn R. Gardner, adult TCK and author of Between Worlds: Essays on Culture and Belonging and Worlds Apart, A Third Culture Kid's Journey

"In "Incredible Lives and the Courage to Live Them", Rachel Cason does just that. Many who grew up as TCKs feel they live in different "compartments". Depending on where they are or who they are with, they may be their "African self" or "British self" or "Chinese self" or any other type of "cultural self" at any given moment. While this type of cultural adaptability is a great skill to have in our globalizing world, it can leave adult TCKs wondering exactly who they are personally. Many also do not fit the common characteristics associated with TCKs and wonder if they belong to that community either.

Rachel reminds us that no matter where we grew up or what our passports may say, our stories are a flow from beginning to end often containing countless paradoxes along the way. While sharing common feelings and experiences she and others have known, Rachel also gives room for each reader to be "all of the above" or even "none of the above" and still belong. Many readers will find great relief and new hope that they are not alone as they dare to explore and embrace the totality of their lives without having to squeeze it into any else's preconceived box. It is a book of hope and will bring healing to many who struggle as I did with wondering how with such an incredible life, there can be places of quiet sadness and grief for no apparent reason. A must-read for adult TCKs of all backgrounds."

Ruth E. Van Reken, co-author of Third Culture Kids: Growing Up Among Worlds, 3rd ed., author of Letters Never Sent (her story!), and co-founder of Families in Global Transition

"Sometimes you read things that connect with you deeply, or make you feel seen, perhaps they put you at ease, or give fresh perspective on what you thought you already knew. In "Incredible Lives and the Courage to Live Them", Rachel has done all of this and more. Rich with useful imagery and insight, this book is warm and inviting. Rachel has woven her ability to open up intellectually what many of us feel intuitively into each page, and in manageable portions invites us to explore more. I sincerely recommend TCKs on their way to adulthood and those who've already moved into adulthood read this book!"

Christopher O'Shaughnessy, International Speaker, Globetrotting Adventurer, and author of Arrivals, Departures and the Adventures In-Between

"I feel like I've read every TCK book out there and more often than not there is a focus on the hard stuff. Rachel tells her story, and invites us to look at our own, with kindness and compassionate towards our selves and our cultures. Her years of work as a therapist to third culture kids make this book uniquely thought-provoking, tender and tangible. Add it to your TCK book shelf immediately!"

Jessi Vance, founder and CEO of Kaleidoscope, a community that celebrates the TCK journey

"Dr Rachel Cason's book invites you into the joys and challenges of the TCK life in a way that feels intimate - as if you're sitting across from her with a cup of tea having these conversations. Her clinical experience bolsters her narratives without taking away from the warmth and practicality. Rachel has brought to the TCK community a fresh perspective in the form of a beautiful collection of essays that separately dive into various parts of the TCK experience while collectively painting a beautiful picture of what it is like to navigate growing up globally mobile. If you are an Adult TCK, parent of TCKs, or anyone who loves and cares for TCKs, this book needs to sit on your coffee table so you can regularly flip to a chapter and absorb the many nuggets of wisdom and insight."

Lauren Wells, CEO of TCK Training, author of Raising Up a Generation of Healthy Third Culture Kids, The Grief Tower, and Unstacking Your Grief Tower

Acknowledgements

The idea for this book came from a dear friend from my childhood. Tineke Bryson has been a generous reader and encourager of my writings for a number of years and suggested they could form the basis of a larger work. Tineke, as a skilled word-smith yourself, this suggestion meant so much and I'm so grateful you took the time to imagine this book.

To the gifted writers, authors and TCK professionals who took time to read this book with a generous eye and give me such encouraging feedback, I'm so grateful. Your words came at a time where really needed them. Thank you. I must also thank Danau Tanu, who dedicated significant time and energy in reading through my manuscript, and her helpful and thoughtful comments as well as personal feedback were formative in this final publication.

I must especially give thanks for Tanya Crossman's generosity and skill in fine-tuning my writing into a form that could best communicate my heart's offerings. With a gorgeous combination of pragmatism and cheerleading you have been both a vital and joyful part of my journey to publication. The fact that she then also gave her time to write the foreword for this book means so much to me. Your own contributions to the world of Third Culture Kids are remarkable, and I'm so grateful for your time and encouragement in my work here.

In both encouragement and design genius I owe so much to Darren Hendley. His inspired vision and execution of the front cover is one that I feel so excited by and that is so representative of his significant gifts in this area. Without his abilities in formatting and knowledge of the technical elements of publishing I would have been utterly lost. I'm so completely grateful for your daily love, care and relentless belief in me.

I have long felt lucky to have family who have not only tolerated my curiosity for and challenging of anything "status quo" but have actively encouraged it. They have made it safe to wonder, to ask hard questions, and have loved me throughout. Thank you, both for my childhood *and* for how you've made space for me to deconstruct its impact.

And finally, this book simply could not have been written without the brave souls who reached out to me to share their stories. Their courage and determination to want more for themselves – more understanding, more hope, more love – has inspired the following pages. I'm especially grateful to those Third Culture Kids whose stories directly propelled me to write the pieces on "Languages – those we've loved, and lost" and "Third Culture Kids and Repatriating Well".

You are so beautiful. Your stories are so precious. And I'm so grateful to have walked with you for a while.

Foreword

Each Third Culture Kid's life story is important, mapping a unique journey. They might not map tightly to the experiences of people around them, but that does not mean the TCK journey is impossible to decipher. It does however mean that many TCKs feel alone in the work of understanding their own life stories.

I know this all too well, not only as an adult TCK myself, but also having formally interviewed hundreds of TCKs – and listened to the stories of hundreds more – over my nearly two decades of work in the global mobility field. Helping TCKs feel heard, understood, validated, and empowered to move forward underpins much of the work that I do.

Dr Rachel Cason is a precious gift to the TCK community. She is an expert cartographer of TCK life stories, helping us chart our journeys. She points out the landmarks and geography of a Third Culture upbringing, and how their effects ripples through our lives – the ways our journeys have curved around that hill, followed this river, or languished in that desert.

I have followed Rachel's blog for years, and have regularly been encouraged and inspired by her writing. I share her writing and insights with my own readership, including many TCKs and parents of TCKs. She offers personal insights and deep emotional resonance as she shares her own TCK world, having grown up abroad, then settled in her passport country as an adult – now raising a child who cannot comprehend how different Mummy's childhood was. She also brings a depth of insight that comes from serving as a therapist to many other Adult TCKs.

This book feels, in a way, like journeying through a season of therapy with Rachel. She empathises, offers helpful insights, asks provoking questions, creates space for personal reflection. The chapters flow not in a rigid structure but conversationally, sometimes referencing or revisiting a previous conversation to bring additional thoughts or add depth to an idea.

Every TCK needs these conversations in their life – needs someone to create this space, to act as cartographer, tracing lines across the topography of their childhood experiences, seeing the journey held in those stories. Someone to acknowledge how our journeys mark us.

In working through this book – slowly, gently, with space to reflect – we can become that someone for ourselves. As we read we engage with Rachel both as our guide and also as a fellow TCK on the journey. We gain the beautiful opportunity to trace our stories together.

"We are not alone," we begin to realise, "we have walked some of the same paths."

That understanding, that empathy – and the validation that goes with it – is exactly what every human being needs. We all need to be seen and known. From there, we can journey inward and onward – going deeper, learning more, embracing challenge. In the safety of understanding, we can start growing into the people we want to be.

Tanya Crossman
Author of Misunderstood: The Impact of Growing Up Overseas in the 21st Century

Contents

It's lovely to meet you…

I'm so glad you are here. I'm so glad to be able to "meet" you in these pages. There is no other you like you and you are just so welcome here. In case I haven't had the privilege of meeting you in person, I would like to give you a sense of who I am and what you are about to encounter in this book.

I am a Third Culture Kid. I was born and raised in Niger, West Africa, with a short year in France when I was about 13. I was raised by missionary parents and, like many living within these organisations, my mobility pattern was about three or four years in Niger followed by one year in my passport country for "furlough." And so it was until I was 16, when my parents decided to cut a four year block short by two years and "return" to England, where we settled for the foreseeable future.

I had a foot in a few different cultural worlds – mission, secular, whiteness, expat, England, France, America (due to the dominant culture of the mission), Niger, home-school, international school – and I danced between them for 16 years. And then everything stopped. The arrow juddered to land on England with a stillness that was completely foreign to me. Moreover, I was foreign to "them": unbelievable, unfathomable, incredible. Then a new dance began – the dance of the adult TCK.

This dance took me to university, studying Sociology. Through academic study of society I began to make sense of my story. I had the wonderful opportunity to continue my studies and focus my PhD on Third Culture Kid identity, sense of belonging, and relationship to place. The process of hearing so many other TCK stories was transformative. I heard patterns echoed between them and me that coalesced disparate experiences of uniqueness into a coherent Story – one that told me that what often felt like a personal struggle was actually part of a collective experience.

My immediate goal was to get through a successful completion of my PhD, but a longer term and more meaningful goal began to form. The experience of listening to TCK stories exposed me to the alchemical process that storytelling had for my participants. Telling their life story was often a new experience; we typically tell mini-stories, truncated chapters with heavily translated or curated portions depending on assessment of our listener's point of reference. Because I structured these as "life story" interviews rather than asking them to "tell me your TCK story," I heard the whole sweep of their lives – but crucially, so did they.

As my TCK participants told their stories, they heard themselves – really heard themselves. They heard not only their narratives of present-day struggle, but also the context and landscape in which they had developed. Personal failure or blame lifted into a broader view of the systems and cultures which formed their sense of self. Well-worn narratives of self were transformed into something more nuanced and containing more hope.

And so Life Story Therapies was born – a significant moment in the life of this adult TCK – in April 2015. I had completed my doctorate and now had the opportunity to offer what I'd heard TCKs telling me they needed: space to tell their stories, the support of someone who shared their experience, and hope they could continue their stories from a place of agency and power. I was so excited, so nervous, and so convinced that this would have made a massive difference to me as a 16 year old coming to a "home" that wasn't, trying to figure out how to live well in the stillness that faced me.

Which brings me to introducing this book to you. Over the past seven years I have been blogging my thoughts, experiences and questions about the Third Culture Kid experience on my website, explorelifestory.com. Sharing my thoughts this way has in itself been a journey. Like many TCKs, I prefer to have a clear view of my audience. My ability to chameleon depends heavily on my ability to gauge the expectations of my environment, which means I need feedback. Like any performer, I feel most at ease when I get immediate feedback on how I'm doing. Writing on a blog is a little like jumping into the abyss of the unknown. Will there be rainbows and unicorns at the bottom ready to greet me with hugs and cupcakes? Or will there a more frightening prospect – puzzled lack of interest at best, or people horrified by my nonsense at worst?

Yet blogging has, in the very way that it's been terrifying, offered me the opportunity to take ownership of my thoughts. When a chameleon is denied an environment to adapt to, she gets the chance to see what colour she is – underneath. I began to hear my own voice, daring to share her thoughts unapologetically, risking rejection and alienation but hoping that if someone read my words, they would feel heard and less alone. But in order to offer real connection and empathy, I had to show up as my own "colour". This tormentingly difficult process has resulted in 168 blog posts to date. As I wrote, I began to hear from other Third Culture Kids that my words had some resonance for them. My words were inviting other TCKs to respond and interact and engage with their own stories – to feel less alone, to share in a community of marginals, to feel the burden of particular struggle lift as they heard the voice of collective experience.

Over seven years I shared these thoughts from my life as a TCK and my observations as a TCK therapist. When a friend suggested these words of mine would collate well into a collection for a book, I decided to believe her – my latest leap into the abyss of the unknown. And so, this book.

I hope you find the chapters that follow welcoming, stimulating, comforting, thought-provoking, and challenging. I hope you find in its pages ways to make more sense of your incredible story, and ways to validate your own experiences with new waves of compassion. Even as you read the thoughts of this TCK therapist, I hope you become more intimately acquainted with your own thoughts around the story you have lived so far, the story you tell today, and the story you want to write for the chapters still to come.

I am so glad you are here. Let's begin.

What a Third Culture Kid is and Why You Can't Be It Wrong

How do you know you "count" as a Third Culture Kid? You know, a *real* one?

This was raised as an issue for my doctoral research on TCKs – how would I define them?

This question has caused me agonies – of self-reflection, academic analysis and a heart-wrenching realisation that such definitions can be another experience of exclusion and "othering" for so many. This chapter has been written and re-written and this final form is largely thanks to the prompting of Danau Tanu and her dedication to that critical tension between clarity of concept and inclusivity of experience.

In the first, we have to thank the Useems for their observation of the children of Americans working in India in the 1950s. They developed the term "third culture... as a generic term to cover the lifestyles created, shared, and learned by people who are in the process of relating their societies, or aspects thereof, to each other. The term third culture kids, or TCKs, was coined to refer to the children who accompany their parents into another society".[1]

Later on, David Pollock expanded on this definition to note the implications of this childhood accompaniment, noting that "the TCK frequently builds relationships to all of the cultures, while not having full ownership in any", thereby finding that "the sense of belonging is in relationship to others of similar background".[2] In Pollock and van Reken's revised "Third Culture Kids: Growing Up Among Worlds" in 2009, they highlight four common characteristics of TCKs that I have seen ring true for my TCK clients; TCKs grow up often seeming physically different from those around them, they are aware of impending repatriation, they are often deemed to have a privileged lifestyle and have a certain system identity present in their constellation of identities.[3]

But these characteristics don't all ring true for all those identifying with TCK stories. White Americans growing up in Belgium are not necessarily physically different from their peers, for example. Others may have less of a sense of impending repatriation if growing up in a country to which they have citizenship rights. Still others may be perceived as less privileged than other TCKs or host country peers at their school or in their community, and some TCKs may have parents who worked for local businesses, affording them less "system identity" than others.

Personally, I've found myself leaning a lot on this system identity as an indicator of the kind of TCK experience someone may have had. This is most clearly distilled into the question: "What took your parent outside their passport country in the first place?" This is often a matter of career, and I see many similar experiences shared around living situations, school attendance, lifestyle and values that coalesce around certain parental occupations, and the system cultures of the organisations that orchestrate their family's experience of mobility. Yet this is not a universal predictor by any means, and it's just the start of the TCK story.

And then the other variables at play in our TCK stories? What about the length of time abroad? Age of first move? What about if time was spent in one parent's passport country, but not the other's? Was that still "abroad"?

What if the TCK grew up attending international schools? Local schools? Was home-schooled? Went to boarding school? Boarding school in the passport country while parents were still working abroad?

Then there's the nuanced experiences of TCKs themselves. Assumptions abound around compound/expat accommodation, multilingualism, status, and access to material security. Assumptions reverberate around books and on the internet about how grateful TCKs should be for their experiences in other countries, about how they must miss those people and places.

What about those TCKs who never left a country but still crossed cultures domestically, via reservations or communal living? Do they "count"?

What happens as a TCK gets older? Are they no longer a Third Culture Kid? What happens to their identity now as an adult Third Culture Kid?? Do they have to keep behaving in a particular way to keep their "membership"? Keep travelling? Stop travelling? Work abroad? Work in their passport country? Work in an international field? Work with different languages? Find their purpose on a global scale?

There are so many lists online claiming to enumerate the ways "you know you are a TCK." These tend to list a set of behaviours that are felt as signs of belonging, indicators of TCK identity. I've always struggled with them. It felt to me that there was a gatekeeping element to this kind of list. All meant in fun and as an offering of solidarity, but I hear too many stories of TCKs who felt they somehow didn't count as "TCK enough". The pain I heard in these stories made these lists feel less fun and more exclusionary.

There have been other offerings too – alternative titles that attempt to describe the shared experience of mobility or global experience: global nomad, adult Third Culture Kid, global citizen. Personally and professionally, I keep to "Third Culture Kid." For me, this definition keeps the "Kid" element central. Not because our identities are frozen in time, located fixedly in our childhood years, but rather because it keeps the focus on *when* these significant shared experiences occurred, in that childhood. It also refrains from putting ages or length of time down in specific terms, which is great because WE get to interpret the significance of our experiences to us. It is our story, after all.

So here is the crux of my understanding of what it means to be a Third Culture Kid: we are TCKs not because of who we are *now*, but because we shared similar experiences around mobility, transition, and cross-cultural living *then*.

This means we don't have to interpret those experiences similarly to continue to "count" as TCKs in our adult lives. So I offer this list of my own:

I believe you are a Third Culture Kid if you spend what feels to you like a significant part of your developmental years outside your parental culture, and if...

... you hate travelling OR if you love it.

... you speak multiple languages OR if you are monolingual.

... you feel you have shared experiences with your immediate family OR if you feel the 'odd one out' amidst them.

... you felt at home abroad OR if you felt like a perpetual alien there.

... you feel alien in your passport country OR if you feel at home there.

... you feel kinship with other TCKs OR if you feel kinship with people who have more settled stories.

... you wouldn't trade your experiences abroad for the world OR if you totally would.

... you feel drawn to make a global impact OR if local connections are what you long for.

We can be different Third Culture Kids. We can have different experiences from one another and still claim TCK identity, if that is helpful to us.

Lists of observable behaviours can be helpful in reminding us we are not alone, but when our claimed identities begin to make demands on our behaviours or our preferences, then we have an identity we can feel anxiety and shame about. We can fail at performing the identity 'properly'. Don't we have enough experiences of this already?

Not English enough.

Not Chinese enough.

Not white enough.

Not Black enough.

Not woman enough.

Not man enough.

Do we need to add "not TCK enough" to that list?

Your TCK-ness is defined by the early mobility of your developmental years – not by how you experienced that mobility or how you responded to it later in life. The shared experience of mobility, transition and cross-cultural living is often what magnetically pulls us towards each other. But we are not all alike. Even as we have shared experiences, even as we may share how these experiences have impacted our bodies, our self-concepts and our orientations to the world around us, our stories are our own. Incredible stories that bear your own unique fingerprint. And nobody gets to tell you your fingerprint is "wrong".

Third Culture Kids, you can't fail at or lose this identity.

No ifs. No buts. You belong.

[1] Useem, R. and Cottrell, A. (1996). Adult Third Culture Kids. In: Smith, C. D., ed. Strangers at Home, New York: Aletheia Publications, pp. 23-4.

[2] Definition of TCK by David C. Pollock in The TCK Profile seminar material, Interaction Inc., 1989, 1. In: Pollock, D. C. and van Reken, R. E., 2009. Third Culture Kids: Growing Up Among Worlds. Revised Edition, London: Nicholas Brealey Publishing, p. 13.

[3] Pollock, D. C. and van Reken, R. E., 2009. Third Culture Kids: Growing Up Among Worlds. Revised Edition, London: Nicholas Brealey Publishing, p. 17-8.

Why We Need
to Tell Our Stories

Whenever I start working with a new client, I explain that our first session will be two hours long, rather than the usual one hour. This gives us time to walk through the whole of my client's story – from the beginning to the present day. It is not uncommon for me to hear, "Oh gosh, I won't need that long!" And yet when the time comes, every minute of that precious two hours is needed. And sometimes more.

We aren't accustomed to telling our stories this way. We are more likely to drop elements of our experiences into conversations, offering some context here and a little detail there. Our stories are also likely to be told out of order – prioritized instead by whatever is happening in our present to trigger an echo with our past, requiring a piece of our story to step forward and explain.

And this is what our stories do: they explain who were, where we have come from, and how we have arrived where we are today. But for explanations to be effective, they need an audience. And they need an audience who understands.

Many of us have painful experiences of feeling misunderstood. This may be because of cross-cultural expectations or assumptions we have been caught up in, or because of our own society's misunderstanding of our situation or experiences. Either way, we can feel burnt by misunderstanding and hesitant to risk another attempt to tell our story. And yet, the need to tell it remains. We need to tell our story to make it real, restore our authorship, and invite connection.

For those of us with complex and fragmented stories, our stories can take on an unreal quality in our minds. They won't be told in a straight line, change language halfway through, and our own character goes through frequent and dizzying metamorphoses. For some of us, certain chapters only seem to make sense to certain audiences and so we learn to compartmentalise for coherency's sake. Finding a listener, an audience with people who will accept and understand all the pieces of our story, is crucial. The telling of our story to such an audience helps make the story real. The words that narrate the fragmented elements of our selves ground our story and bring it from mythology into reality. Telling our story makes it real.

The narrator of a story holds all the power of the piece, guiding the story, and setting its tone. Which voice narrates our story – our own, or that of someone else? How many of us feel our stories have been told for us? By our parents? If our parents worked abroad, perhaps by the sending organisation? Where is our own voice in the telling?

Telling our story is an opportunity to use our own words to narrate our own experiences. While we may lean on well-worn stories from previous narratives, we have a new invitation to forge new sentences and suggest new interpretations. We can become our own authors again, positioning ourselves as writers of the story, rather than having our story run away from us.

Choosing our audience is important here. It is important to protect tender places in our story from indelicate and insensitive prodding. The worst culprit for this is sometimes our own selves. We reject our own experiences where they shame or worry us. Where we have felt rejection from others we can take this and turn it on upon ourselves. We are the author, but we are also our own first audience. Do we receive our own stories compassionately? Gently? Do we connect with our own story, accepting all its chapters with love and hopefulness?

We need connection. Connecting with our story connects us to our self. But it also has power to connect us with others. Where we have felt ourselves to be "terminally unique" we may overlook universal experiences of loss, excitement, marginality, and transition that are in fact shared by many whose stories look, on the face of it, entirely different from our own.[1] Where we can use our stories to invite connection, sharing of experience, our sense of isolation dissipates and we invite relationship into our next chapters.

We need to tell our stories. It can feel risky, painful, and vulnerable, but all the good stuff – groundedness, power, and relationship – lie on the other side of the telling.

---

[1] Bennett, J. (1993). Cultural Marginality: Identity Issues in Intercultural Training. In: E.M. Paige, ed., *Education for the Intercultural Experience*. Maine: Intercultural Press, pp.109–136.

Your Story
Makes Sense

Some of the most painful things I've felt, and heard expressed to me, are the feelings "I'm crazy," "I shouldn't be feeling this way," or "I don't make sense."

To feel you are incomprehensible, unreasonable, unfathomable is just so lonely. And frightening.

Many Third Culture Kids have lived lives of staggering contrasts: poor here, rich there; face fits here, but language fits there; materially or experientially "lucky", but experiencing so much loss.

These contrasts can confound our attempts to make sense of our Selves. We tell our Stories haltingly, constantly watching for cues that our listener "gets it". More often than not, we learn that somehow our Story alienates, alarms, or confuses the people around us.

And so we learn to partition the whole into discrete chapters – this one makes sense over here, that one makes sense over there.

We learn who we are in relationship. The inter-personal acquaints us with the intra-personal. So it follows that the more fractured our relationships, the more fractured our sense of self risks becoming. If our story doesn't make sense to others, we may begin to feel it doesn't make sense to us either. We may think, "I don't know why I feel this way", but there will be a reason. There is always a reason.

We have a tendency to split head and heart. The mind speaks rationally, and emotions speak – well, emotionally.

Except it doesn't always work this way. Emotions are clues. If we are to detect sense in the story, we have to honour the significance of the clues.

In so many who-dunnits, blundering policemen fail to notice the significance of seemingly irrelevant clues. Luckily for us, and the plot line, a detective often comes along who makes sense of these clues. Crucially, this detective assumes there is sense to be found in these clues, even when they appear senseless.

You feel your emotions for a reason. There is always a reason, even when the sense of it is not immediately apparent. This is where the magic is. When "I don't know why I feel this way" becomes

"I feel *this* way" we can deal with the feeling – either through understanding ("I wonder where that came from, when else have I felt like this?") or through compassion ("What do I need, feeling this way?").

Both new responses assume the feeling has sense, takes it seriously, then moves you on from the feeling. Frustration with the feeling, or denial that it has any sense, tends to lead us more into stuck-ness: "I shouldn't have this feeling, I don't know what to do with it".

Your story may be full of seemingly contradictory beliefs, experiences, and feelings. Yet it does have sense. I guarantee it.

And if your story makes sense? So do you.

Déjà vu and glitches in the Matrix: when TCK worlds collide

Do you remember the Matrix films? The films follow a hero through a dystopian reality check where, among other things, he learns to pay attention to moments of *déjà vu*: "glitches" in the world around him. These glitches were often a subtle sense of something not quite right within its own frame of reference, such as seeing the same person cross the same road twice within a few moments. These glitches were clues to a world hidden behind the apparent reality.

I see glitches too. My moments of *déjà vu* find me looking at a scene, or participating in an event, and being suddenly thrown beyond it to another time or place. My gaze can soften and pass through time and space to my other life, where something like this – and at the same time, very unlike this – has happened before.

A recent moment of *déjà vu* happened on a visit to a bit of nearby countryside. The trail ran up a hill with a stunning 360 degree view. Others were doing the same climb and little clusters of people congregated there, just for the view. A moment of peace and beauty, and shared appreciation of England's green glory.

Standing there, a wave of nostalgia hit me hard. I suddenly felt sad, close to tears, and filled with an unexpected and forgotten longing. An old, familiar feeling to many Third Culture Kids. Homesickness.

I was suddenly longing for dunes. I was thrown back to the times our community abroad climbed the dunes together in the early morning, reaching the top and standing in awe at the view. The longing for a landscape I can no longer reach fills my eyes with tears even now.

On one level the glitching felt intrusive, incongruent, and so inconvenient! The truth is I am here, in England, with people I love, *now*. I want to be here. I am enjoying the day. I love the view.

But it is also the truth that I loved another view first.

And so I glitch. And it's lonely, because how can I share this? How can I share the double vision I am experiencing without wrenching those in my company from the present joy? How can I share my inexplicable sadness without communicating discontent?

Gently. Oh so gently I can hold the wave within me. I can give it boundaries, explore it, and validate it. This wave cannot consume me for I am the wave and it is me. I am nostalgia personified. I am two worlds in one. I can flow between them and hold them both. Two truths together.

Then, secure in my compassion and care for both of my landscapes, I can share my glitching – gently, without discontent – trusting that those I am with care more for me than the view. They can hold my experience as different from theirs. I am allowed to be here *and* there. I can ask this of them.

I am safe in these moments of *déjà vu* when I trust my vision as true. I *can* see both worlds and they both exist – real in their own ways and with their own power.

In the Matrix films, the hero has a terrible choice. He must choose which world to commit to, which reality to invest in.

Reality can be less dystopian than this. As otherworldly as my dune visions seem, they were real – they *are* real. I can affirm both worlds. I can commit to myself in both.

I'm not glitching. I'm remembering all of me.

Languages – those we've loved, and lost

To speak is to be – at least in my world. I'm a verbal processor and I swear sometimes I don't know what I'm thinking until I speak it. In social terms, we often don't feel we exist until we are heard and understood by the world around us.

Babies know this first. Of course, they exist as beings before they speak words we understand, before they share our language with us, but they are born as noise-making beings. They cry. They babble. They communicate. And their constant efforts to communicate pay off. We hear them, we validate their efforts, and they eventually learn our language and begin the process of "joining in".

And what of Third Culture Kids? Language is one of our "identity props", borrowing from Goffman's theatrical framework of identity expression.[1] (I find identity props so helpful that I'll talk about them again in later chapters!) An identity prop is a "thing" – be that behavioural habit, physical object, personal characteristic, skill set, or yes, language – that helps us communicate an identity more coherently. For example, if I am playing Hamlet on stage, at some point it would help to have a skull to hand for the famous "Alas poor Yorick" scene the play is known for. If I am trying to communicate that I'm "not from around here" and that I feel culturally French, it would help if I had some identity props to hand to back up my claim. I need French books in my home, skills at French cuisine, some knowledge of France the country, and yes, some French language skills. After all, who grows up and spends part of their time in France and comes away without speaking French?!

Well, lots of us.

Don't get me wrong. Many Third Culture Kids grow up multilingual. Being able to speak the many languages of our host countries is often one of the markers by which we are invited to identity ourselves as TCKs. However, many of us did not leave our host countries with their languages.

This happens for many reasons. One reason is that many of us attended English-speaking international schools in our host countries, and local language contact may have been limited to a class we attended once or twice a week. Another reason is that those of us who lived in areas with established expatriate communities might have encountered limited time and opportunity to connect with locals, thereby limiting how familiar we felt with local languages. Or perhaps we experienced a host country language as an early language – even our first, our mother-tongue – but subsequent moves meant we lost it.

We may also have felt reluctant to connect to the local language in the first place, perhaps inhibited by observing our parents struggles with language or culture. It can be hard to want to invest in that which we perceive as stressing our loved ones. Or, we may simply not have felt gifted linguistically, and found it difficult to pick up multiple languages!

For those of us who lost languages or felt we never gained them in the first place, we can feel robbed of the prop we need to make our stories make sense to our audience. I often hear TCKs speak regret or shame over feeling they lack a linguistic claim to a culture or identity that is nevertheless significant to their story. I experienced this as a young child, when classmates wouldn't believe I lived in Africa because I was white. When they demanded I "speak African" to prove it, I couldn't; I could speak no African language with any fluency that helped me to make sense to my peers. Others experience this as adults, when they feel the missed opportunities that fluency in youth could have given them now, as well as wishing they had the language skills to "prop up" their claims to cultural affiliation with their host countries.

What about our mother tongues? I already mentioned the sting of losing a host country language gifted to us from babyhood – assumed to be an "extra" rather than a main character on our identity stage. But what if the mother tongue all expect to hear fluently – our national language(s) – is deemed wanting by our audience?

A Korean TCK raised in English-speaking American schools may well find themselves criticised for their mother tongue expression in Korea. We can lose our languages due to a kind of "language imperialism" that exists in our international schools. This can lead to our language skills, even in our mother tongue, being found wanting by passport country peers or even family members. We can find ourselves speakers of many languages but feeling masters of none. Even where our fluency is established, our accents can betray us as "not belonging".

This can leave us feeling vulnerable regarding some of the identities we lay claim to. Without the props to explain who we are, we can be left feeling like we simply don't make sense, like we are somehow doing our identity "wrong". This stings.

So what can we do?

We can give ourselves permission to speak to ourselves kindly, with grace, about our linguistic identity props. We can remind ourselves how we came to have the collection of languages and accents we do and do so without blame or shame. We can refuse to take on shame offered by those who feel we "should" speak a certain language.

We can remind ourselves that the languages we lost are still out there. We can fill our ears with radio stations in that language, fill our bookshelves with grammar textbooks and our favourite children's stories in these languages. We can create space in our lives for the longing for languages we love, even if we feel we can't claim them as our own.

We can grieve the languages lost, or never gained, and the relationships (and potential relationships) that were lost with them. We can acknowledge language as one of the many things we have said goodbye to.

We can give ourselves permission to speak despite the misinformed expectations of our audience. We can speak, haltingly perhaps, but nevertheless with insistence born of our conviction that we have things to say.

[1] Goffman, E. (1956). *The Presentation of Self in Everyday Life*. New York: Anchor Books.

Where Trauma Speaks, We Need to Listen

I watched Gabor Maté's documentary on trauma, "The Wisdom of Trauma," when it first launched and, like many others, I was profoundly touched by it.[1] His assertion that all it takes for someone to be traumatised is for them to feel overwhelmed and alone in their feelings especially struck me. It was a late night of watching, and in the small hours I found myself weeping at the combined relief and hope that his words and experience offer. Relief, because his approach validates my own approach to working with human pain, and hope, because of the healing power of relationship that he demonstrates.

I've run out of fingers to count the number of times I've heard clients say some variation of, "nothing *really* bad happened to me, I don't have any reason to be finding things as hard as this". It breaks my heart every time.

You aren't struggling for fun. You aren't feeling alone for your own personal entertainment. You have *reasons* for the coping strategies that have gotten you this far, however much you may be wanting to distance yourself from them now, and the fact that these coping strategies developed at all speaks of a situation that was challenging for you.

Trauma is not a scale that justifies our suffering as "big enough" to explain our need for support. Trauma is not the things that happen to us. Trauma is the learning we absorb that...

... we aren't safe.

... we aren't protected.

... we aren't enough.

... we are alone.

Trauma is a rupture of our vital, life-supporting trust in people, the world, and in even our own trust in self.

I often tell my clients that working through trauma is like a kind of exposure therapy. In exposure therapy, we slowly allow ourselves to be exposed to the very thing we fear, in order to rewire our brain to learn that this thing is not the threat we believe it to be.

With a fear of spiders, we might begin with being able to tolerate mention of the creature, working up to being able to look at a picture, then a video, then being in the room with one – and on we go until we can hold one without our body going into fight, flight, or freeze mode.

So it is with emotional trauma. The only way to heal is to work with that fear of relationship rupture, to engage in relationship – trusting that not all relationships will overwhelm us, and to be able to reach for ways within our own selves to mitigate the sense of aloneness that hurts so much.

TCKs I work with are often carrying echoes of trauma – either because of overwhelming living situations in childhood, or because the emotional culture of their homes or sending organisations alienated them from feeling "enough" somehow. A lot of us learnt to secure a sense of relational safety through adaptation, accommodation, and appeasement – with a dash of self-blame as a protective measure. The trouble with this coping strategy, however, is that it makes relational safety conditional. The TCK has learnt and continues to assume that acceptance in relationships is earned and contingent on "getting it right" or "making them happy with me". For this reason our trauma can give us a lot of pain whenever we try to attend to our own needs instead of others'. It hurts so we can learn to hate it, kicking out against what we have come to see as our weakness, our fear, our irrational behaviour patterns that make it hard for loved ones to ever feel truly close to the "real" us, whoever that is anyway!

Despite our longing for safety, many of us are caught in a relational cycle, where we find ourselves hurt again and again. In Gabor's framing, as I understand him, the wisdom of trauma is that it carries with it a deep truth about what we still need from relationship – those needs of safety, protection, acceptance, and accompaniment – and that these needs are valid and we can work towards meeting them.

What might change if we were able to stop treating our trauma like the enemy, instead seeing it as a clue to our still unmet needs?

Until we understand these needs, it's likely we will keep looking for them to be met in ways that don't serve us.

The wisdom of trauma is speaking. Are we listening?

---

[1] Lee, S. (2021). *The Wisdom of Trauma - Dr. Gabor Maté.* [online] Dr. Gabor Maté. Available at: https://drgabormate.com/the-wisdom-of-trauma/.

Strategies in Seasons of Change

How do you, as a Third Culture Kid, feel about change?

Change can be a sticky topic for Third Culture Kids. We have already lost so much. We can learn to fear seasons of change, having built an enormous data set of changes that brought us grief, changes we didn't choose, changes that felt like a tidal wave of loss.

Saying that, many of us also fear stability – we chase change, pushing and cajoling it to be change we now control. During change we notice we operate well: we feel strong and competent here. Stability and longer-term commitments make us feel trapped, boring, or offer the faint unease of, "I think I'm doing this wrong." I suspect stability unnerves us because we believe stability is simply change that hasn't happened yet.

We grow up believing change is a constant to be counted on. As a result, we often develop a highly vigilant approach to change. Our highly sensitive TCK apparatus senses changes in the atmosphere and begins to activate our 'change response' systems. For some of us, this looks like an uncanny ability to predict political or economic patterns, flight price changes, or market changes in our field of work. For others, it looks like a heightened empathic ability that notices every head turn or curl of the lip in our vicinity, quickly able to size up office politics or family dynamics.

At times our sensitivity to the seasons of change gives us a sense of power. We often have plans B, C, and D ready while those around us are still in denial that plan A just isn't working. We find ourselves heading off conflict, managing relationships effectively, adapting to the emotional or practical demands of a new season as easily as we would put away our summer coat and pull out our winter one.

What I find though, working with Third Culture Kids, is that we underestimate the stress that all this change sensitivity puts us under. When we are rolling out our contingency plans and adaptations, I invite each and every one of us to remember that the apparent ease with which we do this is proof of the practise we've had, not how little it costs us.

Indeed, on the contrary, many of us had our change sensitive strategies fried when we were young. We were overwhelmed by change after change or uncertain expectation after uncertain expectation, or simply because lack of guidance and support through these changes left us doubting our own ability to survive them. So we are often limited to two response systems in these situations: one, panic; and two, resistance in the face of change.

The first strategy can often spiral us into fear and depression, a feeling that all we love is lost. It is accompanied by shame because TCKs "should" be good at change, which adds a special layer to the despair. The second strategy can isolate us from loved ones or, frankly, anyone who seems okay with the new change. Their okay-ness registers as a rejection of our experience of fear and loss, and for so many of us this is a massive trigger harking back to the isolation of earlier childhood changes. To adapt intentionally to the change we face now would be to imply all changes are, and were, okay – and we are often NOT okay with that.

All of this makes sense given our past experiences of change. For some of us, the seasons came around too fast and we weren't equipped for them. If you grow up not being given that winter coat at the appropriate time, you begin to fear freezing when cold weather comes rolling around.

So, how can we soothe our change sensitive systems?

I'm going to offer two methods: one to respond to a sense of impending change that demands we stay three steps ahead, and one to increase our sense of power during change. There is never a one-size-fits-all approach to human need, so I invite you to take what feels useful to you and leave the rest!

This first strategy I call "honouring our preparedness while remembering we probably aren't at threat". Okay, titling things has never been my strong suit! How about "cutting ourselves some slack" instead? When we developed our high preparedness skills, we were probably either living in a situation that left us feeling the need for high levels of independence, or we were experiencing a high degree of threat. I remember the sense of confusion at panic-buying in the early days of COVID because keeping cupboards stocked with three weeks' worth of sustenance had been my norm in childhood, where curfews and *coup d'état* were predictable seasons of change.

My change sensitive system has long alerted me to impending lack by introducing a sense of panic if I feel I've "run out" of an ingredient or I see stocks running low. It is possible to believe my skills of meal planning and thinking ahead protect me from impending doom. What they actually do is avoid me noticing that I now live 10 minutes' walk from a shop that doesn't run out of food, and that I never have to worry about not being allowed to that shop because of a sudden military takeover. The only way of getting my brain to notice that I'm not in threat is to (shock, horror!) let myself run out of tinned tomatoes occasionally, and to do the walk to the shops all the while resisting my internalised shame over "how could I have let this happen!?"

Where this has gotten complicated is that, for many of us, we have been reintroduced to states of threat through our living situations as adults, or by COVID. If we don't keep an eye on flights, border restrictions, and COVID testing policies, we may lose access to our families, for example. This is where it is important to honour our coping strategies, in balance with a practise of noticing where threat responses might be less applicable at other times. It is a balancing act, but by introducing nuance to our assessment of threat, we can begin to moderate our change sensitive systems, and therefore reduce our stress levels.

The second approach we can call "where is my power?" When our systems have been overloaded by change, entering a season of change can trigger an overpowering sense of loss and powerlessness. I invite you to frame this as indicative of your early lack of support through change, rather than of your inherent lack of competence dealing with it. If a friend moving away triggers a sense of loss of friendship and being rejected by that friend, or even a pain that says having friends hurts too much, then we need to both honour past experiences that taught us this and consider where our experience today could be different. What resources are present to us that we didn't have before? In other words, if we didn't have a winter coat to help us through the cold in the past, how can we get one now? This might include talking to the friend, making plans to adjust communication so we can maintain it over distance, or even reminding ourselves how much they mean to us and how the change now doesn't change what has gone before – what our friendship has meant to both of us.

The "where is my power?" strategy for managing seasons of change is an invitation to parent yourself through this time of transition. If a child was facing change, what would we do? We might talk it out, cry it out, create memory books or photo albums honouring what has gone before, create a vision of the change to come, and give them choices wherever possible.

This last is the crux of the matter: so often we felt a lack of choice. That does not have to be how it is today. If a change we didn't choose is coming, how can our preferences shape *how* we engage with the change?

Transition: a moment where equilibrium hangs by a thread – a moment frozen on the brink before the slow tip into change. We've been through so many transitions; we can feel it is impossible to relax into available stability, fearful of what the next change will bring.

What about now? Can we take pause on the brink of whatever season of change we may be facing? Can we hold space to breathe, notice the shifts in our atmosphere, and how we feel in this moment? A moment before the dive, the pause before the next step falls. A warm drink cupped in your hands while you gaze into space for a while, inquiring of your own well-worn instincts, where and how this season of change could serve us – this time.

Moving Furniture, Telling Your Story

I'm really excited to be sitting here at my desk, writing to you. I had a "TCK moment" yesterday when I realised I needed to move all the furniture around in my office to get my writing mojo back. A few hours of mess, one dismantled desk and a big bag of rubbish later, I'm in a much better place. Literally.

One of the reasons I don't ascribe to the integration-based definition of TCKs (that the Third Culture is a kind of hybridisation of the child's first and second cultures) is because of things like this moving furniture "quirk". It's not an individual quirk. It's not exclusively TCK either, of course, but it is a feature of many TCK stories that I hear – a sense of needing change. If there isn't a travel solution to this need then creating change on a more domestic level becomes a regular feature of life.

Third Culture, in my experience, is not simply a case of mashing together or cherry-picking elements from cultures 1 and 2 – or 3 and 4! Instead, Third Culture is more about the creation of something new: a set of behaviours, rituals, and beliefs that are shared between people. A Swiss-Italian raised in Kenya and France is likely to recognise and identify shared "ways of being" in an American German raised in Scotland and Belgium. How can this be if each are simply integrating elements of their passport and host cultures into a particular blend known only to themselves? The fact that so many of us recognise behaviours in people we have *only* shared mobility or sending organisations with tells me our Third Culture is not merely integrative, but *creative*.

And creating is exactly what I was doing last night as I lumped furniture around and explored how to make the room work for me.

How to make it work for me. Me.

Identity is a creative act. It's not something that just happens to us – though there are elements of this, of course, ascribed identities such as gender at birth, ethnicity, age, and citizenship. But these categories of self are fleshed out, attributed meaning, by our creative acts of Self.

To go back to my office space, when I move furniture I'm not simply moving it for the sake of moving it. Yes, on the face of it, I have an urgent need for change, in and of itself. I've lived here nearly a year, a long time for this TCK brain, and the season I'm now entering is summertime – the season of packing and moving in my own personal life story timeline.

But when I'm moving things, the question lying beneath the surface of my actions is "how do I make this space work better for me?" or even more precisely, "how can my space be better arranged so as to help me be more of the me I want to be?" It is absolutely about identity and taking creative control of that identity.

Or should I say, *identities* – because we carry so many. Of course, one of the wonderful things about people in general is social multi-faceted-ness. I fell in love with Sociology because of how it broke down the many roles we play in our social relationships into discrete categories that reveal these different facets of Self. But the trick to happiness (perhaps the whole point of applied Sociology) is consciously making sure they all get to shine.

This can get complicated for TCKs. While more settled people are carrying multiple identities – such as Daughter, Nurse, Friend – a TCK is carrying multiple cultural understandings of how to be a *good* daughter, nurse or friend. Am I going to be a good daughter today by UK standards or Nigerian?

Dealing with the multiplicity of cultural demands can risk a utilitarian approach to meeting these standards, whichever culture I am currently in is the one whose expectations I will try to meet. Adaptation works, right? This typically leads to lovely, positive feedback. But. When we are in a settled space in our lives, one where the cultural expectations aren't changing with sufficient frequency to give voice to all of our multi-faceted Self, we can get restless, stressed, overcome with a sense of failure, or straight-up depressed.

One coping strategy instinctively deployed by many of us is born of our experience of how a shift in environment invites expression of a different facet of Self. In other words, if we can change our environment, we get to be a different version of ourselves. We are physically creating space for ourselves to express the identity we need or want to be in our next chapter.

I've spent years (seven, actually!) focusing on client work. I still do, and it remains the bulk of how I orient my time and spend my emotional energies at work. In the early years I did a lot more blogging and communication work, trying to create clarity about who I was as a life story practitioner, and how I could serve adult TCKs. But when I did that work I felt a lot of tension around it. "I'm not a blogger", I'd tell myself, "I'm not a *proper* podcaster". I carried a lot of imposter syndrome around feeling behind on how many books I needed to read before I could claim expertise in my field.

All of this showed up in how I set up my office. Not to beat up on my subconscious self, but I set up my desk in a way that didn't scream writer. I ignored my beautiful bureau from my Grandmother that does scream "writer" (because "I'm not, really") and had my back to my wonderful library (because of shame around how many books I "needed" to read) and focused solely on making space for my laptop, where the magic of Zoom calls with clients happened.

Then I wondered why I was struggling to inhabit the identities of writer, blogger, social communicator, and expert in the field.

Moving furniture around is a fun behavioural impulse shared by many of us. I believe it's a ritual that leads us to actively engage with an identity struggle: who do we want this room to say we are?

For those of us who grew up feeling our life scripts were handed to us by our environments, this TCK quirk may be one of the most empowering things we can do to imbue our home spaces with our identity. Can we flip the script to invite our environment to tell our story the way WE want it told, instead?

I love my new office layout. I face the door, tucked in the back corner behind my beautiful bureau stacked with stationary and books and paperwork. The wall behind me is bright saffron, reminding me of a West African sun, and how wonderful it felt to impose such a loud colour on my wall. I feel cosy and safe, and lady of the manor as I have my wonderful bookshelves to my right; my eye catches them, and I decide to get excited by all there still is to read and absorb.

My office is now a better place. Better simply because it tells the story of who I am more fully— I am therapist, writer, social communicator, creative designer, and lifelong learner.

What story does your space tell of you?

What would taking creative control of your story look like?

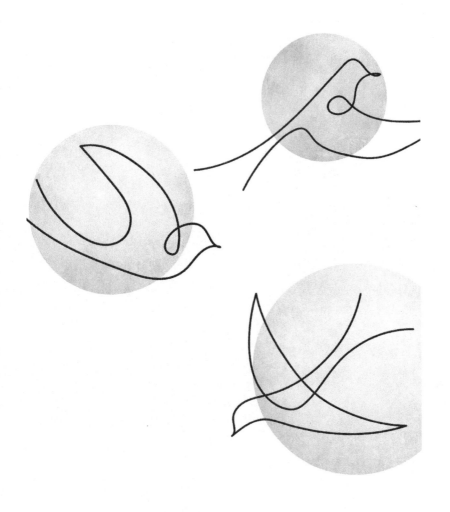

You were never supposed to do this alone

One of the most painful cries of the heart I hear is, "Shouldn't I be able to handle this on my own?"

This question speaks of so much shame, so much self-judgement: the double-whammy of pain, if you will. One whammy, that of the pain of whatever challenge/experience is being faced, is enough. But here a second piles one: that however painful this is, I shouldn't be finding it so hard. I should be able to handle it – and handle it alone.

Alone.

Maybe you have felt alone for a long time. Maybe you feel alone because you really don't have people around you. Or perhaps you feel "alone in a crowd" – you have people around you but feel out-of-step with them and their perspectives or experiences.

When we've had early or prolonged experience of alone-ness, we can get good at handling things on our own. We change our own lightbulbs, manage our own decisions, sit with our own emotions.

And yet.

While we may have adapted for self-sufficiency, we are not designed for emotional island-living. In particular, there are some areas of psychological and emotional processing that we cannot be expected to work through alone.

In the beginning, in an ideal situation, we learn we are acceptable and worthy of love. We learn this from other people. We learn this as children, young children. Our parents first model this belief for us: that we are inherently marvellous. Even in our strops, anger, grumps, and failures. In our earliest months and years we need other relationships to demonstrate we are worthy and acceptable.

Ultimately, the idea is that we can integrate these positive beliefs our significant others display into ourselves. We learn if others think we are acceptable, we can believe ourselves to be acceptable. A foundational belief such as this is a kind of talisman, blessing, protective bubble: it is a deep well of self-acceptance we can draw from throughout our lives, grounding us in our own intrinsic worth even when we meet those people who do not treat us as though we are worthy.

However, even where our parents did a wonderful job of filling up our "well" of self-acceptance, other life circumstances can poke holes in it. Frequent moves, shifting cultural expectations, ruptured relationships, trauma, loss, grief – all of these and more can signal to us that maybe we aren't as worthy as we thought, or hoped. Maybe we aren't worth sticking around for, being interested in, having time or money spent on us. We learn others are more worthy.

Wherever and however our well of self-acceptance was breached, we need other relationships to help us plug the holes. We need to learn that people do stay, do care, are listening, and are not repelled by our anger, grief, and fear.

We were never meant to learn our worth alone.

We were also never supposed to figure out how to handle conflict alone. We learn this through practise. Friendships wax and wane and we learn how to distinguish between those worth working through and those we need to extricate ourselves from. Except sometimes we don't. Sometimes we didn't get great friendship modelling from our families, or we moved around so much that we are best acquainted with the 'honeymoon' phase of relationships – only the good, not having the time or longevity to run into conflict. Or perhaps we learnt to jump in deep and quick with people, approaching relationships as an all-or-nothing process with little room for the ambivalence and ache cause by slights, hurts, and conflict. Perhaps life events have left us approaching relationships from a "beggars can't be choosers" perspective. When we feel vulnerable to losing people, we don't tend to feel confident risking any upset to them.

Where we feel tender around conflict, we need gentle practice. We need relationships that stick around long enough, get deep enough, and are with people different from us to invite healthy conflict, discussion, and disagreement. We need people to practice this with.

We were never meant to figure out how to navigate conflict alone.

And what about our identity? The big "who am I" question? Our sense of self is initiated through interaction with others. Are people laughing at my jokes? I guess I'm funny. Do people ask me to hang out? I guess I'm likeable. Do I get good grades? I guess I'm smart. There are lots of experiences that can confuse and complicate this process. Perhaps we had caregivers who gave inconsistent feedback – smart one day, stupid the next. A common experience for people moving between communities or cultures is that the feedback we get can change dramatically between groups of people. This group value this skill I have. That group thinks it's inadequate or irrelevant. In this city/country people think I'm funny, in that one people think I'm rude. In this school I'm smart, in that school I'm behind my peers.

Receiving lots of mixed messages while growing up can result in feeling like you are trying to piece together a sense of identity using puzzle pieces from different boxes! Lots of partial images that just don't want to join up with other ones. Lots of not fitting together. Lots of not making sense to anyone looking on.

We develop a sense of who we are with support, with people, in relationship. What got muddled up in childhood we can unravel and clarify in adulthood – but we were never meant to figure out who we are alone.

We need feedback, affirmation, validation – supportive witnesses. This is not weakness. This is just how it was always supposed to be.

If you are reaching for support, community, help – you are exactly where you are supposed to be. If you can, shed the shame of needing support. If you can't, reach for someone who will remind you that you were never supposed to go through this alone.

We need other people's voices to find our own, not to mirror but to model how valid it is to speak! Where people have wounded us, we need other people to enter into our healing. We need to be in relationship with people to be in relationship with ourselves. And that's how it was always meant to be.

"Shouldn't I be able to handle this on my own?"

No. And you were never meant to.

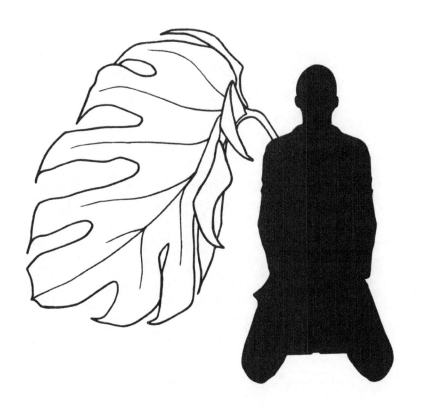

Another's Story is Sacred Ground

In my mind's eye a memory floats into view: a visit I made to the King of the West African town I lived in as a young child. My mother, who was home-schooling us at the time, had taken me and my younger sister to admire the local palace architecture. We were looking up at the crenulations, discussing how we would describe this in a write up later, when a couple of men approached us.

My mother greeted the men and, after a brief interchange, she relayed to us (I had lost my grasp of the local tongue by this point – my birth tongue, an ever-present loss) that we had been invited to greet the King, who was in fact in residence that day. Slightly stunned, my mother gestured to us that we were to follow and take her lead.

Upon entering the room, she observed the King resting on a throne, while the men of the court were prostrated on mats around him, as was the custom. My mother promptly sank to her knees, prostrating herself and touching her head to the floor in respectful greeting. We followed suit.

The poignancy of this memory lies for me in the awareness I held, even then, that we had been granted a peculiar honour, and in all probability due to our whiteness, but that my mother was not going to let that interfere with her attempt to signal her total submission to the rightful author of that scene, the King who welcomed us.

The message I came away with that day was that when you have been invited into another person's story, you take a knee. You are on sacred ground.

Another person's story is sacred ground, and this belief is absolutely core to what I do.

Before I can ally with anyone as they make sense of their story, I have to become a hearer of their story.

The fact that I've written that last phrase in the passive voice makes me momentarily uncomfortable. I recall the countless English essays I received back covered with the red penned critique, "passive voice, correct!"

But I won't change it here.

Why stick with "a hearer?" We more often refer to people as "listeners', people who "actively listen'. Why am I stubbornly refusing to correct my phrasing?

Because a hearer of stories is engaging in intentional passivity.

In taking a knee to the King that day, my mother demonstrated intentional passivity. We had been invited into another's story, and we took a knee.

If we are listening, truly listening, we acknowledge that we enter another's story upon invitation. We acknowledge the rightful author in front of us, and we submit to their authorship. It is an unearned honour to receive, to hear, to bear witness to another's story. We are invited to enter their world for a time. And we do this on our knees. There is no other position to take.

Take a knee.

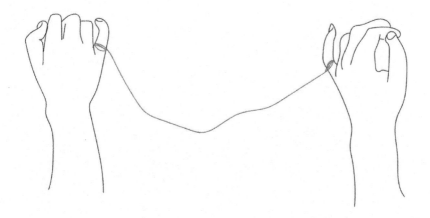

Third Culture
Kid Relationships:
Attachment &
Trauma

I have been increasingly convinced of the importance of understanding attachment theory and its relevance to Third Culture Kid relationships. In this theory, Bowlby proposes that the way we experience relationship in our first few years draws up a blueprint for our later relationships.[1] If we experience consistent responsiveness from our caregivers, we develop "a secure base" from which we build a sense of the world around us as generally reliable and responsive to our needs. If we don't experience this from our caregivers, our beliefs about ourselves and others is rendered insecure.

One way to establish what our early experiences (pre-memory) of attachment is to look at the way we engage in relationships now. How do we do relationship in our present day lives? Do we feel secure in our relationships? Or perhaps we feel anxious about them – never quite convinced the affections we receive will continue. Perhaps we feel avoidant in our relationships – aware of our need for connectedness but hesitant to ever be truly vulnerable in relationship, instead prioritising independence.

Many of my clients have experienced trauma of one kind or another. Trauma may be understood as disordered emotional or behavioural functioning as a result of severe emotional or physical stress. Some trauma is easily recognised: the result of earthquakes, civil war, a car accident. Other trauma origins are more subtle but may include experiences such as routine and frequent loss, linguistic and/or cultural alienation, family dysfunction due to internal or external stressors, and physical illness that limits and complicates what would be seen as expected day-to-day functioning.

Why am I linking attachment and trauma? Well, because there is such a thing as "attachment injury" which, according McLeod, is when trauma occurs within the context of a relationship.[2] I've been pondering the implication of this with particular reference to my work with Third Culture Kids, who have experienced many of the more subtle traumas I mention above. They also often experience relational challenges later in life.

It wasn't easy to write that last sentence: Third Culture Kids often experience relational challenges later in life. And yet it is so understandable that this should be true! The repeated losses, the early care-giver relationships left behind, the continued movement in adulthood complicating grounded connection to place and people – and the belief etched onto many of our hearts: "Everyone Leaves."

So, where does attachment injury or trauma of any other kind feature in our story? I hear it most often showing up as self-blame. "If only I was stronger, more spiritual, less messed up", and yet, if it is true that certain challenges are commonly felt across a particular demographic, we have to look beyond personal weakness for explanation. The data simply demands another explanation. Instead, I sincerely believe that your challenges are not merely the result of personal failings but are instead normal responses to extraordinary circumstances.

Where does this leave us? It leaves us in the uncomfortable position of inferring that certain elements of the Third Culture Kid experiences as essentially traumatic. These experiences are traumatic because they interfere with the abilities of large portions of the TCK population to connect securely in their adult relationships.

Of course, there is hope. Where we learnt self-blame, we can learn self-compassion. And where we find compassion, we find acceptance, which is what nurtures the most enduring change. We can change behaviours learnt through painful experiences. Change is, after all, what we do best.

---

[1] Bowlby, J. (1988). *A secure base*. London: Routledge.

[2] McLeod, S. (2022, Aug. 18th) "What is Attachment Theory? The Importance of Early Emotional Bonds", *Simply Psychology*, Attachment Theory | *Simply Psychology*. [online] Available at: http://www.simplypsychology.org/attachment.html.

Performing Identity
& the props we use

How do you feel about the idea of "performing identity"?

For many people, performance is associated with faking it, inauthenticity or even, drama. It can feel jarring to consider identity as performance.

And yet, how many of us have a distinct feeling of masking when with other people, especially people we feel won't understand or accept the less predictable elements of us?

My hand is up.

I have a tendency to slip into particular "characters" that have eased social interactions in the past – I play the fool, the quiet watcher, the intellectual, the mum. In each role I am reading my audience. Have they bought into my performance?

When I was studying identity at university, especially the ways in which it is socially constructed, I was intrigued by the tension observed between the reactive performance of the self I felt others expected and the times when I intentionally chose to write my own performance.[1,2]

There is something empowering about entering a room, a conversation, a relationship, with some notion of the identity *you* are wanting to communicate, to perform. This is THE performance – the Real One – the truth of the Self.

There is something wounding if our performance is misunderstood, disbelieved, or even rejected as implausible.

Enter, the props.

On a stage, props are used to back up the story being performed. A character tells us he is a pirate and we believe him all the more when he appears in pirate hat and eye patch, wielding a cutlass. The props "prop up" his performance, his identity, and make sense of the story he is telling about himself.

Identity props serve the same function for our identity performances – and are critical elements of successful communication of self to others. (I talked about identity props once already, near the beginning of this book, when discussing the role language plays in our sense of Self.)

An identity prop is anything that connects you to your story, either with its presence, or by the way it allows you to "do" your identity. The way we decorate our homes can act as a nod to who we are and where we have come from. The languages we speak, the foods we cook, the hobbies we love, the plants we root into our garden, the incense we burn – all are opportunities to intentionally communicate our stories.

Identity props are a way of bringing forward experiences that mattered to us in the past, at other times, in other places. We gather them in, finding avenues for their expression in the ongoing adventure that is Identity.

Some of us have lost props along the way. I have lost languages, relationships, memorabilia, collections of ornaments, photos, gardens, hobbies, access to the foods I love. Because of the symbiotic relationship of many props with the place they are "from", it is natural to feel that moving away from that place means we lose the prop. This is one reason many of us feel so scattered; we've left parts of ourselves in many places.

Yet one of the wonders of the identity prop is that it can be reinvented, rediscovered, resurrected. Don't misunderstand me, loss is loss and much of what we lose can never be restored. We honour that, we grieve it. But then we find ways to continue to acknowledge the significance of that loss in our daily lives. When we lose a loved one, we grieve, we mourn. And then we put up pictures, visit places of memory, light candles, and create rituals that help us honour them. In this way, we bring the relationships of our past into our present and make space for them in our futures too.

Identity props offer the opportunity to bring the significant experiences of our past into our present and future chapters. Performing identity is *doing* identity. We can take classes in languages we have lost. We can scour the internet for recipes we thought were out of reach. We buy plants that remind us of distant childhoods.

In using identity props we both honour our own stories but also offer a mechanism for better communicating our stories to the people around us too. We share food from our stories, we invite people into our homes full of art from our host countries, and we share of our Selves with them.

This is the beauty of performance for me. It is no fakery. Rather, it is truth communicated on such a universal level that the complexity and subtlety of the story connects, rather than alienates. It is most helpful, however, when *we* are writing our own script.

---

[1] Goffman, E. (1956). *The Presentation of Self in Everyday Life*. New York: Anchor Books.

[2] Goffman, E. (1961). *Asylums*. New York: Anchor Books

Third Culture Kids
& Hidden Loss

I know I'm lucky. I know I've had a privileged life, full of wonderful experiences. In fact, I sometimes describe myself as a collector of experiences, like others collect precious gems. But I have collected one experience along the way that weighs heavy: hidden loss. Perhaps you, too, recognise this experience.

I am a Third Culture Kid. And with every move I made, I gained – and lost.

I lost languages.

I lost friends.

I lost the ability to trust in continuity of affection and relationship – I came to believe that relationships would not last.

I lost homes.

I lost intimacy with my extended family.

I lost educational opportunities.

It can be hard to acknowledge this loss. It can feel a lot like whining. A phrase I hear a lot in my TCK clients is, "I struggle so much but, after all, I am fortunate – I know". Awareness of our own privilege can easily block our ability to acknowledge the presence and significance of loss in our lives.

Another block to acknowledging the losses we have sustained is fear of casting blame on the people or institutions behind decisions that kept us moving, kept us from staying. Acknowledging our pain might feel tied up with needing to know where to assign responsibility for it.

So, the pain lurks on, in the back of our minds, in the dark and lonely corners of our hearts. Unnamed, unwelcome, unacknowledged.

Why name loss? Why acknowledge it?

Because loss makes its effects felt even while we try to dismiss it.

When we try and catch the rising tears, unbidden and frightening in their ferocity – loss is there. Another relationship comes and goes, reminding us that people always leave – loss is there. Hesitancy to enjoy even a few moments of peace and contentment, because we cannot trust this feeling to last – loss is there.

Naming our losses does not need to detract from our gains. Acknowledging the pain of the hike does not need to sour the beauty of the view. No either/or, just a fuller picture. A more real picture, one with shadows as well as highlights. A story with depth, grounded in our actual experiences, rather than in the ones we feel we were supposed to have.

I believe the notion of 'no blame pain' can be useful here. While understanding and acknowledging the impact other people's decisions on our lives is important, we can lay that down for a moment if it is getting in the way of noticing our own pain. There are many times when we have felt losses at the hands of those we love, and this complicates our ability to acknowledge that hurt even occurred. It may well be that blame for certain losses is entirely appropriate; laying responsibility at the doors of those inflicting pain is an important part of many healing journeys.

But sometimes, the burden of this is enough to stop us even acknowledging our pain, for fear that doing so will require us to have to 'do something' with it. No blame pain says: the pain is simply there. Let's just acknowledge it is there for now; I feel loss and pain. I lost things/people/places and it hurts.

What are your hidden losses?

Do you feel lurking, hidden, unacknowledged loss?

What impact is this unspoken loss having on your life?

Can you coax your pain out of the shadows, to be seen – perhaps even comforted?

Love is… scary

I did not expect to write that title. It just came out as I began to type. The last decade of my life has been dedicated to the pursuit of deep, meaningful, and (wait for it...) *lasting* relationships. I grew up as a Third Culture Kid, like many of you, and mobility was my stability. I knew that I was good at initiating friendships, but long-lasting ones were less comfortable for me. For a start, they were unfamiliar. Either they left or I did – this was the rhythm of my life. While this sounds painful, I had built up some pretty sturdy callouses. Goodbyes weren't that hard for me and I was confident in my ability to rebuild social connections at will.

I had been raised in a community that saw this ability to let go and rebuild as a skill set and, until recently, I adopted a similar perspective. I acknowledged that I had other skill sets missing – the ability to maintain friendships and engage in small talk, for instance. But I wasn't too concerned by these. "I'll adapt," I thought, "I'll learn." So I did. I learnt how to do friendship-building over time, and in place. I learnt how to stay, and how to build community. I thought I was doing great! But I did not account for how I would feel about these friends. And I did not account for how scary those feelings would be. I did not account for love.

In reducing friendship to a set of behavioural rituals and routines, I had focused on data rather than experiences. Data said "this is how people make and keep friends, and how people perform friendship". Experience crept up on me. Experience of love and intimacy and mutuality said, "but what if I lose them?"

For a brain hardwired to predict and adapt to loss, relational attachment is frightening. Attachment implies dependence, and that dependence threatens the very survival of a soul that has learnt to live in perpetual transit. Scary.

I have been scared many times over the last few weeks.

Sharing in the gut-wrenching grief of a friend in a time of terrible loss. Scared that another's pain can hurt me so, so deeply.

Hearing the joy of friends in pregnancy and with new-borns and realising I will be able to watch their kids grow up. Scared because these children don't have to love me or even tolerate me, as I am not "family". And yet I love them so much already.

Being "seen" and understood by a colleague, unexpectedly and unwaveringly. Scared because I thought I was so good at being invulnerable.

Being hugged spontaneously by a dear friend and being taken aback by how much that meant to me. Scared because I have never needed friends before.

It has never felt so good to be so scared.

Can Third Culture Kids be Racist?

Something uncomfortable I noticed during my research with TCKs in their host country was the presence of what I'd describe as casual, covert racism. The kind of "I love this country but its people are…" or "They shouldn't club together to speak (any language other than English) when here at school/in the dormitory". This latter I described in my thesis as language imperialism. That's a fancy academic term for racism. It's just racist.

I'm aware I am being direct, and that this might be uncomfortable. I wonder if I should have cushioned this more, opened with some affirmations that TCKs are cosmopolitan, tolerant and open-minded. Then I remember that there is a fair amount of that content already out there. What I'm observing now is a much more painful reflection – that the Third Culture Kid experience is not in fact a vaccine against intolerance or against racism.

I am a white adult Third Culture Kid. I grew up as a privileged minority in a majority Black country, but the critical element of that sentence is *privilege*.

My whiteness gave me protections, exclusions, and considerations that my host country peers did not have access to.

My whiteness gave me precedence in early childhood games, where my preferences were deferred to.

My whiteness made me the status of powerful Helper, rather than the grateful Helpee, in endless social interactions.

My whiteness contributes to my racial bias, my own racism.

Being a TCK does not make me immune from these. My time in Black host countries does not protect me from the insidious effects of privilege. I remember a conversation about what constituted racist behaviour when at school here in the UK. My (white) friends were asserting that the important piece was that we should not see colour, that we should render this irrelevant in our interactions. I was horrified by what felt to me to be identity erasure, and I was fairly outspoken about it. Someone in the group said what I was saying was racist, and before I could reply another friend jumped in, asserting, "She can't be racist, she lived in Africa!"

While I was gratified to be defended, I remember feeling puzzled by the nature of the defence, and how convenient it would be to just let that stand as true. In fact, to my shame, I did – happy to "win" the protection of my white peers in that moment from an accusation of racism. But I knew. I knew that I had just as much potential to be racist as the next person, perhaps more. The fact was that I had grown up in a community where status was highly demarcated by race, perhaps more so than in the communities where I now lived in my passport country. The associations between race and power were not lost on my young mind.

Racism exists even within our most multicultural of communities. We have to listen hard where our privilege deafens us. We have to listen. And learn. And fight racism. Even and especially from within ourselves.

The Struggle in the Doldrums: when TCKs stand still

Despite our many and various differences, one of the universal challenges I've seen adult Third Culture Kids encounter is the struggle of stillness. Ours is a childhood characterised by movement. We moved, the people around us moved – and while we moved through all the usual changes and stages of child development, we lived them out on a global stage that rotated us through different cultures and landscapes.

Stillness beckons many of us in adult life. For some, geographical stillness features only for a season because we find that movement continues to suit us in adulthood. Others find themselves having needs best met by a geographical commitment. It is always frightening, this time when we stand still longer than we are used to, when sameness looms and we can't decide if the stability that continuity offers is worth the sense of confusion it seems to bring.

How often do we meet these periods of stillness with a sense we are simply not designed for the occasion? After all, many of us feel at our best in movement. Give us change, transition, a new project, a crisis even, and this we know, this we are good at. This ability can serve us well. After all, life is full of transitions, if not always geographical, then relational or career-focused transitions lend wind to our sails. We can harness these changes to build our skill sets, collect experiences that develop and challenge us, and even offer reassurance and comfort to others along the way.

But what happens when the winds of change drop, and we become still?

There is a passage in C.S. Lewis's *The Voyage of the Dawn Treader* that goes some way to expressing the fear that the doldrums bring to sailors. The wind drops, the sails hang useless, and a slow awareness comes upon everyone on board that there are limited resources on this ship. A ship's entire purpose is, after all, to take a crew from place A to place B – without movement it cannot achieve what it was designed for.

For TCKs, staying still can bring on the unease of the doldrums. We can find ourselves looking around at our crew of portable identities, wondering how to assign a captain when no new land is in sight. We can become painfully aware of just how hard *staying still* is.

Staying in relationships with the people I am already in relationship with. Staying with work I am already working well in. Staying in a home that is well established and functioning exactly as I need to it for the life I am already living. Staying in place, because I am at home here and have everything I need and more. Staying.

The stillness is uncomfortable. Unsettling. Full of false starts as unneeded adrenaline tries to prepare me for winds of change that don't come. Staying can be a struggle.

Yet the struggle holds hope. Hope that the struggle will stretch trembling muscles into stronger ones. Hope that staying might, just might, offer an alternative adventure; the adventure of building a whole new skill set – that of Staying.

The struggle of the doldrums is real. It is just as much a part of our TCK story as any other – and it holds so much Adventure.

---

[1] Lewis, C. S. (1955) *The Voyage of the Dawn Treader*. Lion Publishers

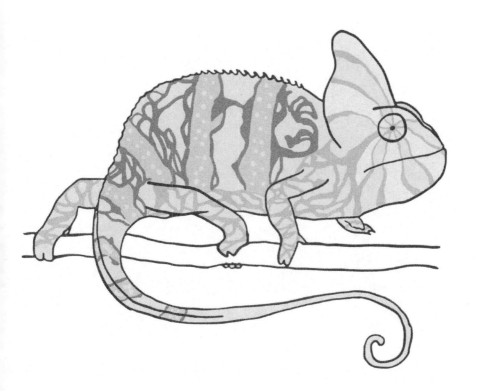

Chameleon
Confessions

Hello, my name is Rachel and I am a chameleon. Like many other Third Culture Kids, I developed early skills of observation and adaptation. I watch, I listen, to learn how to belong. I tried to learn the right colours of spoken and unspoken rules that are my passport to acceptance and validation. Perhaps, like me, the seeking of validation became your life's work too.

But a chameleon is more than colour-changer – it is also the supreme watcher. Eyes spinning in opposite directions, it has 360-degree vision. So do we, hyper-aware as we are of all the various interest groups surrounding us. We spin, scoping out the opinions, the demands, the competing expectations of both individuals and groups, trying to find one we can home in on: one set of expectations we can camouflage to, adapt to, belong to. We spin, seeking acceptance. Surely somebody somewhere will affirm our existence, our beliefs, our choices? After all, successful adaptation is successful living – surely?

Why do we watch so carefully to determine the next "right colour"? It is so tempting to see our adaptations as skilful – a nifty little trick that keeps us able to move between different worlds. This reading fails to acknowledge the fear that is behind our spinning eyes – the fear that motivates our colourful camouflage. I don't chameleon for fun. I do it so I won't be eaten alive.

That's the why. What now?

I am practising noticing another feature of my chameleon self – I have legs! To be fair, anyone who has watched a chameleon move knows they even do this tentatively – rocking back and forth in a three-steps-forward, three-steps-back manner that mimics leaf movement (another safety mechanism) – but it *can* move. This is the crucial piece. As a child, we had limited choice over the environments we landed in, and just set ourselves to focus on adapting to the landscape in front of us. We couldn't use our legs.

But now, we *can* move towards those environments we decide we prefer. The tricky bit is that we don't necessarily have a clear sense of which 'colour' environment we actually want to be in. To paraphrase the famous words of *Alice in Wonderland*'s Cheshire Cat, "if you don't know where you want to go, it doesn't matter which road you take." The biggest reason we might struggle to know the road we want to take is that we aren't clear about the destination we want to arrive at. Choosing a destination might invite uncomfortable feelings of disloyalty. We might feel betraying our own preference makes us too vulnerable to rejection or, under the imperative to fit in. Or we may not have exercised the muscles that help us to notice what we like and what we don't like.

Do you know what colour a chameleon goes when it's angry? I only know because some classmates once carried one to the desk of our head teacher back when I was in high school, and that chameleon was hissing mad – understandably! An angry chameleon goes dark coloured – this one was virtually black. This chameleon knew this was not the environment he wanted to be in. Perhaps you have similar clarity about where you *don't* want to be; you know which environments make your eyes spin with high vigilance and where you have to work really hard to colour change. But what about where you want to be?

A chameleon does not lose its colour changing abilities simply by finding an environment it can thrive in. Those adaptive strategies are built in, but that doesn't mean it wants to have to use them constantly. My chameleon confession? I'm learning that some colours look better on me than others. I'm learning that some environments bring growth in me whereas others feel limiting. And I'm learning I have legs that, however tremulously, have the power to get me to the spaces (and even help me build the spaces!) best suited for me to thrive.

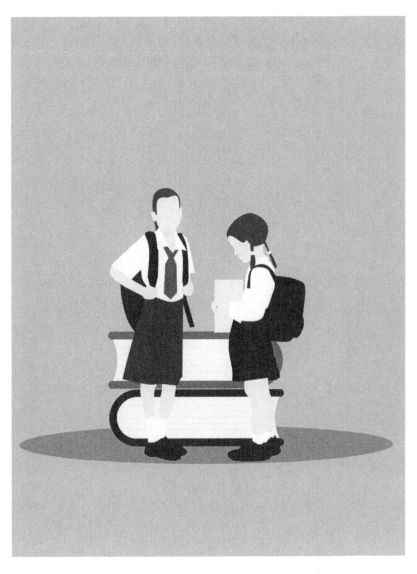

Boarding School Syndrome and Third Culture Kids

There is an article in popular circulation entitled: "The Long Term Impact of Boarding School". It makes for uncomfortable reading.[1] The article expounds on Joy Schaverien's research and experience working with ex-boarding school students, and the development of what she describes as a "boarding school syndrome".[2,3]

This article is unequivocal in its belief that the boarding school experience is harmful to children, and that this harm extends into their adult lives. It equates the separation of the child from the family unit to a bereavement, made all the worse due to repetition of loss. The writer describes boarding school children as without love, alert for rejection, and homeless. The pain of separation may disrupt "narrative flow", as children's emotional attachments are disrupted. It is noted that the rupture of the family unit can reconfigure sibling bonds; compensating "for the loss of family and the significance of the sibling group continues into adult life as a sense of belonging is maintained." The article stresses the presence of trauma so deeply felt, even into adulthood, that it becomes embodied with mental and emotional pain displaying in a range of physical symptoms.

I repeat: uncomfortable reading. Uncomfortable because loving parents send their children to boarding school. Uncomfortable because I have interviewed Third Culture Kids who have fond memories of their boarding school days. Uncomfortable because despite this, I remember one interviewee's description of the "loving abandonment" that continues to haunt his adult life. Uncomfortable because while I tend to steer clear of any sweeping statements about one parenting choice over another (it doesn't do to make a philosophy out of personal life choices), this article has reminded me of my own research findings and the echoes that resonate between them.

My fieldwork in a small international school noted that dorms tended to be run by white Europeans or Americans, no matter how international the demographic of the student population.[4] I observed what I described in my thesis as "language supremacy", where speakers of one language are privileged in some way over the speakers of another, usually following lines of already present power dynamics.[5] In addition to experiencing separation from parents and perhaps siblings also, students in a boarding school with a majority language other than their own may also experience alienation from their linguistic 'homes,' and so from their national identities by extension.

With regards to disrupted emotional relationships, I remember a student expressed how close he felt to his dorm family: "The people on campus were more of a family to me. They were so close to me... and I think that was where I really wanted to live".[4] This is just the kind of disruption of attachment that the article refers to; the student feels more at home away from the parental unit, splitting their identity across the two sets of relationships. Working as I do now with adult TCKs, I see what kind of impact disrupted attachment relationships can have long term, and it's not pretty. When these TCKs "return home", they don't take their dorm with them. They only have their immediate family to turn to in times of emotional need, and they need to have lines of communication that feel open and easy with this family. Instead, what often happens with dorm students is that the transition to their passport country is accompanied by the transition back into the family unit and family routine. This is, by any definition of the word, disruptive. No matter how close the student feels to their family, no matter how loving the relationship, this is a massive transition.

Several students I interviewed also talked about high staff turnover contributing to attachment disruption: "the new dorm parents, they didn't know what was going on [with me emotionally] because they hadn't been there the year before."[4] Shared history – such as conversations, activities, relationships – matters in the development and maintenance of emotional attachments. Where staffing changes are frequent, students lack access to emotional constancy. Another impact of high turnover reported was inconsistency of discipline. Uncertainty around boundaries and consequences would only add to the "alertness" and expectation of rejection arising from disrupted emotional attachments.[1]

Schaverien also emphasises the impact of repeated loss, a phenomenon I identify in my interviews with adult TCKs as "routine loss". In some cases, being separated from parents was more significant than separation from parental love and affection; it could generate not only homesickness but also a fear for the parents' safety. For one TCK of military background, this fear instigated a hospital stay due to a breakdown.[4] Another military TCK recalled "being at times really worried for my parents knowing that if anything happened I wouldn't necessarily hear about it for a couple of weeks... I found out the other day... they were both down with yellow fever... but again I didn't find out 'til years later."[4] Even for those TCKs not at boarding school, the "built-in reality of expatriate organisational life" could introduce routine separation as part of the TCK experience, where one or more parents travelled as part of their work. Where loss can be projected and predicted, children will develop coping mechanisms to respond to "an expectation of being left, which is often unconsciously active in later life."[1] I see the impact of this expectation showing up in so many of the TCK stories I hear, and it breaks my heart each time. There are so many TCKs out there who feel themselves to be expendable.

One coping strategy boarding school students develop in response to routine loss (and which is carried through to adult life) is to compartmentalise. The pain of missing family cannot be endured if felt daily, so they focus on immediate activity, study, and fun. They live so fully in the 'now' that longer term relationships – or the mechanics of maintaining relationships – become complicated or disrupted. "Out of sight, out of mind" becomes a useful tool in this context, though potentially crushingly problematic as TCKs enter adulthood unsure of how to maintain emotional bonds, especially when anticipating potential future absences.

Disrupted narrative flow is another issue that impacts boarding school students, arising from a lack of time markers, such as birthday celebrations.[1] This has not emerged as an issue in my work with TCK ex-boarders, who instead experienced issues around emotional narrative flow. Those I interviewed were often fluent when discussing their time at boarding school, but family life events featured much less often, or were fixed in "holiday mode" – periods of time where students had fewer family life routines to structure their narration. As with all research, the truths that emerge will not apply to everyone equally. If you are a boarding school student or ex-boarder, your experience is valid – whether the issues raised and described by Schaverien (and others) apply to you. One of my ex-boarding interviewees was clear about his close relationship with his parents, saying, "I like some sort of anchoring point... my parents are here [in the same country] so... I can ring them every week. Maybe contact them and meet them twice a week."[4] The trouble is, these are the stories we find easiest to hear. In my experience, TCKs feel a particular need to feel bonded with their immediate family, as they are one of the very few anchoring points to their history. But closeness can be present alongside pain, and emotional strategies developed to aide us in one context could harm us in another.

There are hurting ex-boarders out there and hurting parents too. Boarding School Syndrome may not be a popular concept for many, but for those who need a language with which to express the validity of their experiences, it is a valuable one.

Note: Joy Schaverien writes of boarding schools from a British perspective.

---

[1] Brighton Therapy Partnership (2016). The Long-Term Impact of Boarding School. [online] *Brighton Therapy Partnership.* Available at: https://www.brightontherapypartnership.org.uk/impact-of-boarding-school/.

[2] Summary of Professor Joy Schaverien's seminar on Boarding School Syndrome that took place in Brighton in April 2016: https://www.brightontherapypartnership.org.uk/impact-of-boarding-school/

[3] Brighton Therapy Partnership. (2016). *Brighton Therapy Partnership* | The Emotional Impact of Boarding School - an Interview With Joy Schaverien. [online] Available at: https://brightontherapypartnership.org.uk/emotional-impact-boarding-school/ [Accessed 21 Nov. 2022].

[4] Cason, R. (2015). *'Third culture kids': migration narratives on belonging, identity and place.* [online] Available at: https://keele-test.eprints-hosting.org/id/eprint/1029/1/Cason%20PhD%202015.pdf [Accessed 21 Nov. 2022].

[5] Aneta Pavlenko and Blackledge, A. (2006). *Negotiation of identities in multilingual contexts.* Clevedon ; Buffalo: Multilingual Matters.

Language
Imperialism

I came across language imperialism before I had a name for it. If you have spent time in a multi-cultural, multi-lingual setting, you will have experienced the negotiation of trying to establish a common denominator: the language most spoken and understood. You will have witnessed a group dynamic writhe under the effort to incorporate such "individual" individuals and lend accessible expression to all their tongues. Language imperialism, on the other hand, is when this negotiation does not occur.

Marttinen describes language imperialism less as a group negotiation and more as an authoritative demand. She is speaking especially to school contexts where "non-English-speaking children" are required to mute their tongues in favour of the English language.[1] Of course, this language imperialism could also favour other languages, but it is true that many international schools especially operate in this tongue and "the school demands that the child learn the school language as fast as possible, [discouraging] the use of the child's native tongue."[1]

During my studies I witnessed the informal segregation of students who did not have English as their mother tongue. Students also expressed to me that they were actively discouraged from speaking their own languages in both a dormitory and day student settings, for the "sake" of other students and to help with their own settling in. In my thesis, I wrote:

This "language imperialism", while perhaps seen as necessary for homogeneity and to discourage factions according to nationality among the student body, nevertheless has important implications for that student's home life, relationship with their parents[1], and future relationship with their passport country.[2]

Language is the means by which we think about ourselves, others, and the world around us. Our vocabulary is formed by our language(s), and with it, the expression of our experiences. I'll never forget the sadness of a Polish American student, that she had no one with whom she could speak Spanish. She had spent her primary school years in Spain, and it was her heart language. No one even expected her to need to use this language, as it was not tied to her national identity, but her experiential identity.

Is it possible that language imperialism can damage not only mother tongue identifications, but also heart and host language connections also? Once again, Third Culture Kids seem to confound categorization; even in our challenges we seek to redefine the terms!

More than this, while language imperialism is a structural bias and problem, I have also witnessed a kind of internalized linguistic hierarchy within many TCKs. How many of us who are multi-lingual privilege one language over another? Are we prouder of some of our languages than others? Do some run to a strong social currency?

When we lose a language once dear to us, and fundamental to our sense of belonging – and do not reclaim it – this creates a shift in our identity. We can almost feel the bridges burning and know deep within ourselves that, without that linguistic link, we can never belong there again.

When we are shamed for lost proficiency, we are shamed for who we are now – that our identity now is not "as good as" it was then. When we feel shame about language loss, we feel shame about our identity now, and call it "less than", "reduced", and "lacklustre".

Whatever your language story, I hope it is one negotiated rather than one of limitations imposed from on high.

Language imperialism is a feature of many TCK stories and has robbed more than a few of us of opportunities to connect deeply with the places of our stories. What then is the solution? Revolutions are typically bloody and painful routes to independence, yet I support the righteous indignation often key to the reclaiming of linguistic territory.

Your language, your story.

---

[1] Marttinen, A., 1998. Nurturing Our Students' Native Languages. In. Bowers, J. M., eds., 1998. *Raising Resilient MKs: Resources for Caregivers, Parents and Teachers,* Colorado Springs: the Association of Christian Schools International (ACSI). pp. 305-308

[2] Cason, R. (2015). *'Third culture kids': migration narratives on belonging, identity and place.* [online] Available at: https://keele-test.eprints-hosting.org/id/eprint/1029/1/Cason%20PhD%202015.pdf [Accessed 21 Nov. 2022].

PTSD and
Cultural Variance:
Implications for
Third Culture Kids

This is a big topic that has touched many people's lives, and I by no means count myself an expert in it. However, I am writing about PTSD and TCKs because I keep encountering TCK stories that feature pain and trauma. Especially significant to many TCKs is how hard it is to recognise PTSD or complex PTSD in the context of a life that so many perceive as privileged, and where the incidents or experiences that the TCK experiences may simply not "translate" into their current context. This is where Katariana Holm-DiDio's work highlights something with wide-reaching implications for the TCK world; this is the kind of something that needs to be heard.

In 2016, I was lucky enough to attend Katarina Holm-DiDio's workshop on PTSD at the Families in Global Transition conference in Amsterdam.[1,2] The critical point that I took from Katarina's talk is that our experiences of trauma will be filtered through our own particular cultural lens. Our understanding of our Selves, others, and the world around us is influenced by our cultural world, and this in turn impacts how we express emotional pain and how we heal. In other words, a TCK may express emotional pain in a "language" from their host culture, and these expressions need to be understood for what they are if that TCKs is to receive the support they need.

An understanding of culture bound syndromes can be helpful here. Culture Bound Syndromes are defined as "recurrent, locally-specific patterns of aberrant behavior and troubling experience that may or may not be linked to a particular DSM-IV diagnostic category."[3] Now, just because you originated in these localities does not mean that you will inevitably experiences these syndromes. But they are worth noticing.

Katarina outlines specific examples of culture bound syndromes in her work, including:

In Cambodia, there is *kyol goeu*, or othostatic panic, a "sudden episode of fainting, when the individual often is unresponsive but conscious."[1,4]

In Mexico, Puerto Rico, and other Latin American Cultures there is *ataques de nervios*: an "episode of acute emotional upset" that is "a cultural variation on a panic attack."[1]

Korea has *hwa byuang*: "aches and pains, palpitations, anorexia, insomnia, fatigue, panic and fear of one's death."[1]

Malaysia, Thailand, Japan and the Philippines and some Siberian groups experience *latah*: in which a person is "hypersensitive to sudden fright and is characterised by echolalia, being in a trance-like state and a tendency to follow commands," and "tends to be more common in middle-aged women."[1]

Katarina concludes that these culture bound syndromes are an important example of how health and wellness is experienced and expressed differently in different cultures. Sounds clear enough, right? Except this: TCKs grow up with multiple and, at times, conflicting cultural lenses. A British TCK may identify more closely with Mexican or Cambodian culture. A Cambodian TCK may identify more closely with British culture. Will their symptoms of trauma and distress be recognised by their passport countries, when those symptoms originate elsewhere?

The implications of PTSD and its cultural variances are mind-blowing. Third Culture Kids are one group of many that migrate around this beautiful, and messy, globe of ours. Like others, their early cultural exposures and identifications may bear little resemblance to the cultures they move through and settle into later in life. As such, a clear and sensitive understanding of TCK life stories becomes crucial.

For those of us working with TCKs, it is not enough to understand that a person's cultural background impacts their experiences of both suffering and healing. Therapists also need to become fully aware of the hidden, as well as visible, elements of a TCK's cultural history, moving beyond their current cultural identifications. This is why I work with the TCK's story first, because this context is what makes sense of everything else. Therapists working with TCKs must understand that there will be different health and illness concepts internalised by each TCK, and that these carry variances in understandings about what is typical and healthy, so that we may be better positioned to more effectively support their self-views as they move forward towards healing and wholeness.

For TCKs living with physical or emotional experiences that are distressing, your story holds the key. Beginning with confidence in this we can ask ourselves, "What do the cultures of my story say about expressions of health and illness? How can these help me make sense of my experiences now?" Your story makes sense of all your experiences, and while it's not always easy to tease out the threads it is so important to hold on to this truth: your experience now makes complete sense given your story.

---

[1] Holm-DiDio, K. *Cultural Differences in Post Traumatic Stress Disorder Symptoms and Prevalence*, Iona College

[2] Also at FIGT 2016, Amy Jung kindly shared some resources about complex PTSD, something that may be of interest to readers.

Complex PTSD - U.S. Department of Veterans Affairs

http://www.ptsd.va.gov/professional/PTSD-overview/complex-ptsd.asp

Complex post-traumatic stress disorder - Wikipedia

https://en.wikipedia.org/wiki/Complex_post-traumatic_stress_disorder

Other non-scholarly / unofficial sites are beginning to address this disorder. Examples:

http://outofthefog.website/toolbox-1/2015/11/17/complex-post-traumatic-stress-disorder-c-ptsd

https://www.elementsbehavioralhealth.com/mental-health/what-are-the-symptoms-of-complex-ptsd/

[3] , American Psychiatric Association (2000) *Diagnostic and Statistical Manual of Mental Disorders* (4th ed) Text Revision. Washington, DC: American Psychiatric Association. P. 898

[4] Boehnlein, J.K. (2001). Cultural Interpretations of Physiological Processes in Post-Traumatic Stress Disorder and Panic Disorder. *Transcultural Psychiatry*, 38(4), pp.461–467. doi:10.1177/136346150103800403.

Resenting "Resilience"

Much has already been written about Resilience: how to foster resilience in our children, how it is a good thing, and a predictor of success. I would cringe at the sound of it all. As much as my rational brain knew that the science behind resilience made sense, I recoiled. Odd because, after all, who would want the alternative? Who would want to *not* be resilient? Who wants to crumble under adversity?

Yet I hated what I saw as the "push" to get kids resilient, the privileging of the resilient over those who felt their suffering more keenly. I hated that stories were silenced because their authors "should" have been more resilient and transformed their narratives from pain to positivity – like Rumpelstiltskin's straw turned to gold.

Resilience is a particularly popular buzz word for Third Culture Kids, those children raised abroad due to parental employment, and their expatriate communities. For anyone who has loss or transition built into the structure and fabric of their lives, resilience can be an attractive concept.

And yet I resented Resilience because resilience implies the presence of pain – and I don't want to see people suffering. When I heard people applauding resilience, I heard them encouraging exposure to pain. "After all, it's good for them. They'll develop resilience." Resilience felt like a get out clause – an excuse to not adequately protect children from suffering. Resilience symbolised the abdication of caring responsibility.

I resented Resilience because the image it conjured up was of fatalistic thinking, of a person bracing themselves against a gale, not allowing it to blow them away, but making no gains either. Resilience, to me, was being stuck in perpetual tension and immobility, reaching only for exhaustion.

I resented Resilience because it sounded sad. It sounded lonely and joyless. A resilient person sounded walled up, protected from the bad, but holding out no hope for the good. Resilience meant unwept tears and a British 'stiff upper lip,' an attitude that saw suffering as all there was to life, a person simply trying to make the best of a painful situation.

And yet...

Pain is not something we can avoid. It is true that the suffering of many is heightened by their communities, or even their families. Yes, some of the pain we meet as children could have been avoided. And yes, childhood pain will echo into our present day lives. Pain is a significant part of our reality. Resilience is a response to pain, but it doesn't need to be seen as the cause of our exposure to it.

On a hot day (this is England we are talking about!) I went running with a friend who struggled in the heat. This friend is a better runner than me, hands down. I mean, she does marathons, and runs while pushing her child in a buggy. She is strong. But the heat was knocking her. Meanwhile, while I wasn't enjoying the heat, I was coping fine with it. In fact, I was running stronger than my friend. You see, I was raised in West Africa.

Something in my body, in my psyche even, knew that I could survive this heat, and worse. That sweaty discomfort was somehow familiar, and because it was familiar, I knew I would get through. My friend felt like she was dying, while I knew I wasn't. That is Resilience. We suffered the same challenge, but because I had suffered this challenge before, I knew I could and would get through. Resilience is what happens when we know we can get through. And this is a powerful, wonderful thing.

Resilience is not just a bracing of the self against the inevitable and unending storms of life. Instead, resilience is this sense of power, of ability, of having the resources to get through the storms triumphant. Resilience harnesses knowledge and strength built through previous storms and conquers the present one with grace and dignity. Resilience says, "I survived that loss. I will survive this one. But this time, I know how to handle my grief". Resilience is not immobile. Resilience advances.

Resilience is not isolation and suffering in silence. Resilience is not fatalism. As long as we take the time necessary to notice our strength building, Resilience can be Joy. We can find deep joy in our own ability to connect the past with the present, learn from it, develop skill-sets and rejoice in our own creativity in the midst of challenge and pain. And when our Joy, and our acceptance and delight in ourselves, bubbles over – we connect with others. We are infectious and extend our warm embrace of ourselves to those around us. For all that we thought we couldn't, WE CAN!

I love being wrong about stuff like this. Resilience used to cause me to cringe; it represented a perceived expectation that I should brace myself for life's challenges with stoic courage, courage that doesn't cry. Now, Resilience is power, confidence, and a deep Joy.

It is worth spending a bit of time with the ideas or concepts that cause us to recoil. As we sit in the discomfort, we are challenged to reflect on the reasons behind our revulsion. We are asked to problem-solve and reconfigure our thinking so as to conquer the fears that lie behind our reluctance to engage.

What other ideas, concepts, or expectations do you find challenging: Home? Settling? Long-term friendship?

How would it be if you sat with them for a while?

When Life Goes On... and On... and On

It was a tumultuous time, encompassing bereavements of various kinds, some difficult relationship situations that required careful management, and the madness that invariably accompanies the school holidays. I was struggling. With everything. And my well-worn coping mechanisms simply weren't working. The balls weren't just being dropped – they were pelting me on the way down.

As I desperately searched for understanding as to why I wasn't "managing life appropriately", the answer hit me: life was going on.

You see, I am a Third Culture Kid. The pattern of my life has included multiple and regular transitions, beginning in childhood and continuing into my adult life.

"In one sense TCKs are repeatedly "dispersed" from their passport country, yet in another sense TCKs are dispersed in later life from their TCK (abroad) community, particularly abruptly as a result of graduation or even evacuation in cases of civil unrest or ill health. TCK dispersal then cannot be understood as an interruption to life's normal cycle, rather dispersal constitutes the norm and settledness the crisis."[1]

Typically, when a life change arrived in my formative years, such as moving from primary to secondary school, or even just class years, chances are my whole life would change. I would often be moving countries, too. Difficult relationships developing in my friendship group? No worries, chances are you'll move away soon, or they will.

Life events that demand a complete overhaul of routine and daily life, I can do.

Change is my Home.

But Home was changing. This time, Life was carrying on.

Cue my second epiphany: At the time I had stayed 'in Place' for 3.5 years at the time of these realisations. I had been in my home for longer (in terms of consecutive years) than any other home. The impact of this is that life changes now need to be integrated into Life in Place, rather than being absorbed by a more dramatic Life Overhaul.

Meaning: Life Goes On.

So how can we as TCKs do this without falling apart or running away?

Both of these seemed good options to me at the time! One of the alarming things to me was that my life was becoming an uncomfortable combination of the Mundane and the Novel.

Novel I can do, novel I am familiar with. After all, if a new project or life change doesn't go to plan, I can shrug and say "Oh well, I'm new at this!" But three and a half years in, that phrase doesn't slip so easily off the tongue.

First, we can acknowledge that staying through life change is *hard*! As soon as we stop adding to our stressors by blaming ourselves for our stress, things (miraculously!) get easier. Perhaps, like me, you have never done this before. Perhaps this is your first encounter with staying, ploughing through. So it's okay if it's scary, even overwhelming. Hang in there – practise makes it easier.

Second, we can look around us and learn from those who know how to do this. Find non-TCKs, the "monoculturals" so often decried in our literature, and observe how they do it. We don't need to re-invent the wheel here – though that's somehow a much more appealing thought to us novel-seekers! Instead, find the experts and put those adaptation skills into practice!

Here are two of my observations of how settled people manage lives that go on.

First, settled people invest in relationships past and present. They allow relationships from different times and places to interact, to integrate.

Many TCKs find that relationships get compartmentalised. For some, new relationships are much easier to get excited about than "old" ones. Other TCKs fear the loss of old friendships, because with them one loses precious shared history, and a sense of the Self one was. These TCKs risk spending so much time and energy in the 'past' that new relationships in the 'now' fail to get the time and energy they need to flourish.

Second, settled people expect life to be "normal", and this doesn't crush or frighten them!

Heidi Sand-Hart writes in her autobiography, "I struggle to accept that life won't be as exciting and varied as it was growing up. Realising that "real life" is mundane, even unglamorous at times, is a hard pill to swallow."[2]

Practising the valorisation of the mundane can be a life-long project, but it is worth it. Without it, we can put immense pressure on ourselves and our lives to be extraordinary, whatever form that takes for us.

I have recently taken on the mantra, "What would be the normal thing to do now?" Rather than constricting my perspective, this somehow opens me up to a whole range of choices and feelings that I had previously dismissed. Odd, yet effective.

---

[1] Cason, R. (2015). 'Third culture kids': migration narratives on belonging, identity and place. [online] Available at: https://keele-test.eprints-hosting.org/id/eprint/1029/1/Cason%20PhD%202015.pdf [Accessed 21 Nov. 2022].

[2] Sand-Hart, H. (2010). Home keeps moving: a glimpse into the extraordinary life of a third culture kid. Hagerstown, Md: Mcdougal Publishing.

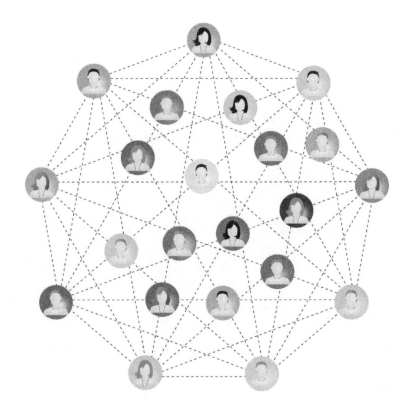

Calculating
Friendship

I am a Third Culture Kid therapist who is also a Third Culture Kid. Which means that I frequently find myself returning to the same tools I share with my clients. Today this tool was a list: a list of my friends.

Let's back up. Through my research, my own experience, and working with clients, I can say with confidence:

Adult Third Culture Kids often find long-term friendships challenging.

This does not mean that the challenges exhibit identically. Instead there are two main characteristics of TCK friendship making.

One: TCKs can go deep, quickly[1].

They are skilled at quickly assessing friendships that are going to be most responsive, and will be "worthy investments". After all, many TCKs moved so often they have an inbuilt aversion to small-talk, aware that friendships need to be established quickly so that they can embed quickly into the new environment and get established before the time to leave comes around again.

Two: TCKs can find adult friendship-making particularly hard.

What emerges in my analysis of many TCK life stories is the link between growing up in "community" and the deep sense of isolation often felt in adulthood. This link is under-explored in many TCK discourses, but provides the key to understanding why adult friendship-making can be so hard for some TCKs. These TCKs grew up in community, where membership accorded belonging, and friendships were multiple and communal.

For those who find themselves in the first group, who find making friendships easy, keeping friends may be the challenge. Their friendships may move through cycles: first there is an overflow of new friendships, new relational opportunities, followed by a period of perceived isolation where the TCK feels alone, with no-one to call on, and loneliness sets in. They are tired of reaching out, and feel an absence of intimacy in their lives, craving that sense of belonging that gives comfort. This is where my list comes in.

This list has two columns: in the first I write down the names of friends who live at a distance from me – both close friendships and ones I would like to see become closer. In the second column, I note down friends who live nearby, again including both close friends and those I would like to get to know better/do more with. Then I note in my diary when I will reach out to these friends.

Someone once asked me if this felt "calculating". Yes, it does. The biggest gift we can give ourselves as TCKs is to dispense with the myth that 'real' friendships will 'just happen.' While our membership in community is no longer automatic, we *can* build it. We can prioritize it, be intentional about it, and yes, be calculating about it.

For those who find it hard to make friends in the first place, we need to find our community locally. Yup, I said it. Local matters. Even if you hate where you are living and can't see that you share anything in common with anyone there. Find a place where you can share an interest with those around you. If you have a hobby, join a group to practise it in community.

If you don't have a hobby, make one up! Who knows, you might end up loving watercolour painting! And if you don't, you might find yourself at the back of the class with another attendee who has no idea why they are there. And you grab a coffee with them afterwards. If hobbies sound too forced, volunteer. If you can't find a group you want to join with, start one. Find people. Find people who like what you like. And find where they are. Then go there.

Then make a list of all the people you'd like to get to know better. Then email or text them. You can do this. You can build a community.

[1] Pollock, D.C. and Van, R.E. (2009). *Third culture kids: growing up among worlds.* Boston: Nicholas Brealey Pub., p. 133

Sensory Stories

I am sitting in my front room (or sitting room, or lounge, or whatever you call it in your part of the world!) listening to the sound of rain thundering against my windows. And I love it. Not the going out in it bit. But the Sound of it.

I was having lunch yesterday with a friend when a similar deluge hit and the sound of the rain on the roof was deafening! But I loved it.

You see, I grew up knowing the sound of rain on a tin roof to be the sound of Hope, Life, and Joy. Rain meant food for the country in which I was raised and, in the desert lands, was not a thing to be taken lightly. The echoes of its significance resonate into my life now. Indeed, fifteen years later, in cold, wet England, the sound is like an echo of Home.

I had a similar experience earlier this week, when I bought some brioche rolls on a whim. The sweet bread doesn't figure in my diet as a rule (through forgetfulness, I might add, rather than any dietary virtue!) but the smell caressed me as I opened the bag.

It transported me to border crossings where we would lean out of car windows to buy loaves of the sweet bread to sustain us on whatever long journey we were on. I have now resolved to buy brioche more often!

A few months ago, I was faced with an old ironing board that was making an unpleasant task (who actually *likes* ironing?) even worse by being ugly and thinly cushioned. I resolved to procrastinate further from the ironing by recovering the board first. My fabric of choice was length of material I brought back from Niger many years ago. I loved this fabric but hadn't found a use for it until then.

Now, while ironing isn't exactly a joy, it reminds me of fabric shopping – the overwhelming array of colours and patterns in another world, that act as a backdrop to so many remembrances.

Rain. Bread. Fabric.

For me, as for many TCKs, our "other worlds" can feel increasingly distant over time, and distance renders them more mythological than real. By finding ways to "join the dots" of our Then and Now, in grounded and tangible ways, we can not only better access our memories, but draw them into our current experiences.

In this way, the echo doesn't fade, but instead resonates with increasing strength and voice.

What precious memories are reactivated through your senses into your Now?

Third Culture Kids
and Repatriating Well

A client shared with me that they went looking for accounts of Third Culture Kids repatriating long term but found little to inform them. This challenged me in more ways than one – first to consider why the narrative of TCK repatriation was so hard to find and second, to ask myself why on earth I hadn't written on this topic myself?!

We don't tend to talk about repatriation as Third Culture Kid adults, do we? Not in a, "I choose this and it's working great for me" kind of way. Something I found while I was reading as much as I could for my doctoral thesis was that there was a pervasive narrative around "returning to the passport country" being not only challenging, but also hopefully temporary. There are voices that even go so far as to suggest that TCKs who settle "back" in their passport countries are wasting their experiences.

I have seen this thought echoed in my work with adult TCKs who feel the weight of putting their global experiences "to good use." They struggle with the idea of settling in their passport countries, and whether living like a local could ever be enough. More to the point, to repatriate and live locally was often felt as a kind of personal failure.

A failure to what? To "make it" as a global expatriate worker, like our parents? To live an extraordinary life abroad, having adventures on a global scale?

But what if it wasn't failure? What if repatriation could be considered an equal option on the list?

If we could consider repatriation as a viable option for our adult TCK lives, then perhaps we could begin to meaningfully explore what we would need to do repatriation well. I need to be clear here: I'm not saying repatriation is a beneficial choice for all TCKs, just that for many who see it could benefit their long term goals, it's often a choice that is layered with shame ("I shouldn't want this") or fear ("I don't know how to do this").

We already have a well-documented transition aid in the RAFT acronym presented by Pollock and Van Reken to help TCKs learn to leave well.[1] They noticed that in all the losses that TCKs faced throughout their lives, a process was needed to facilitate conscious transition from place A to place B.

What we don't have is a process for repatriating well. Here I propose another acronym: ANCHOR.

I personally prefer the idea of being anchored over being rooted. As a TCK who works with TCKs, I feel confident saying that a common fear is that if we settle, we'll never get out again. It's a fear that often leads to charges of "fear of commitment." I propose that this is less a fear of commitment and more a fear of getting stuck in sameness.

Many of us grew up seeing change as something that happens to us, after all, rather than something we can generate for ourselves in a positive way. Anchors can be lifted as well as dropped, and I like this reference as a reminder that using power to settle is not the same thing as dooming ourselves to being trapped in the same spot forever. After all, the fear of choosing "wrong" has led many of us to never drop anchor at all.

So, here is our ANCHOR:

A – Acknowledge

Acknowledge where regular mobility or living outside your passport country may not be working for you anymore. I have heard a lot of TCKs wrestle with a desire for community, for long term friends, for stable financial situations; just noticing where your current life situation isn't working for you can be hard. It is a courageous thing to sit with the pain and sense of lack, but a critical first step toward being able to name what you might want or need instead.

N – Non-judgemental

By this I mean non-judgemental consideration of what you might want for your next chapters. I have heard TCKs express a lot of shame about considering repatriation. We can carry a sense of failure lent to us by subtle messages we have received over the years. "You are so lucky to have grown up seeing so much of the world" teaches us that settling is second choice. "You have such a cosmopolitan and informed worldview because you've experienced so much" tells us that people without travel are less informed, less aware, more "monocultural". "You've lived such an adventure" suggests adventure comes in a limited form, and that people who stay are missing out on adventure.

I have heard more than one TCK (myself included) express fear of becoming like "them" – the settleds, the 'monoculturals,' the parochial living small and mundane lives. This fear can block us from being able to access solutions to the very needs we might have acknowledge needing for our next chapters – because we judge the situation that meets these needs as somehow "less than". Non-judgmental observation of need and ALL the possible options for meeting that need is the way we give ourselves real choices – and I want choices for you.

C – Community

Many TCKs grew up in tight knit communities. The shared experience of being expats abroad often leads to a greater sense of interconnectedness and interdependence for families living outside their passport countries. While this can be a mixed experience for TCKs, it is often the template we carry of what close community looks like. This can be a hard need to meet, as it often takes more time to build this interconnectedness in settled communities than it does abroad. In fact, many of us recall community being more of a landing pad, just "there" by virtue of shared residence abroad, rather than something we saw built up over years.

Because of this, repatriating TCKs need a strategy for building community, one that helps them remember the long game of community when immediate loneliness feels all too present. It is important to make use of the various community groups available to us, all the more accessible due to the digital age, and to join things. We won't find community in all that we join but, like the lottery, "you have to be in it to win it." For many of us who grew up being given positions of leadership at a young age, it is worth observing how comfortable we are "joining in".

We aren't likely to find our local communities full of other TCKs, but the more varied our own interests, the more opportunities we have to meet others with shared interests. Local volunteering, community groups, choirs, interest or hobby groups, or even regular community service offers opportunities to feel connected with the people we share our habitat with. This sense of connection is crucial to the building of community.

H – Happiness

Knowing what makes us happy is a crucial element of successful repatriation. I see a tendency amongst us TCKs to focus on finding our purpose, our life's meaning. All good things, of course, but I suggest that the pursuit of happiness is the crux of making a meaningful adjustment to our passport countries. Daily joys contribute to mundane meaning-making. Finding our new favourite local coffee shop, the best dog walk, a seasonal rhythm to our garden – these are sustaining moments that anchor us where we have decided to settle.

O – Object Permanence.

Piaget's idea about child development was that as a child ages, they begin to grasp the idea that an object being out of sight does not necessarily mean it's gone forever.[2] Can you see where I'm going here? For many of us, especially in our early years, moving meant irreparable loss. Friendships, schools, pets, homes, even languages– all gone, and all it took was a plane flight or two. I often blame my own tendency to forget names to the sense that, in the absence of seeing the person in question recently, my brain assumed they (or I!) left the country and so I will never see them again. The name is archived in my brain and I look heartless the next time I see them. But I am not heartless, I am just accustomed to losing people.

Successful repatriation requires that we remind our brains that parts of our stories set in other landscapes are still ours to claim. We need to remember them, and the 'who' we are in them. We can do this in our homes – with pictures, artwork, the scent of incense, or favourite foods. We can do that by seeking out continuity in how we have learnt to love our landscapes – hikes may move from desert dunes to Scottish highlands, but we are still hiking. We intentionally move from compartmentalised chapters to a stitching together of an ever-expanding life; settled but not stagnant. Our other parts and our other places are not quite gone, we realise, just hidden from view.

And finally,

R – Remember

Remember what repatriation is doing for you. Remind yourself why you want this. Having a clear sense of why you have make this incredible decision to repatriate, to settle, is important. This remembering centres you, encourages you, and motivates you forward as you invest in a whole new chapter for yourself.

Remember your story so far. Remember a new chapter is just beginning. Remember repatriation is a choice, as full of opportunity as any other. And remember the opportunities that you are gifting yourself.

ANCHOR: Acknowledge, Non-judgemental, Community, Happiness, Object permanence, Remember.

---

[1] Pollock, D.C. and Van, R.E. (2009). *Third culture kids: growing up among worlds*. Boston: Nicholas Brealey Pub.

[2] Piaget, J. and Cook, M. (1954). *The construction of reality in the child*, by Jean Piaget. London: Poutledge & Kegan Paul.

The Third Culture
Kid drive to
"be good"

I am currently sat at my desk in a mild slumpy grumpy space. It's because I've eaten too much sugar and drunk too much coffee and now I feel I need a good long lie down. I want to hide from myself, because I'm cross that I over-indulged. However, given that I'm me, I am feeling curious as well as grumpy – why did I do it? Why did I eat and drink more than was good for me? Now I'm getting all philosophical and asking the BIG question – why do we do what we don't want to do, and why don't we do what we want?

I reckon it's because of the stories we carry of how to be a "good person".

You see, my peanut butter cookie fiasco started because though they were what I originally wanted – I didn't put them on my plate. Instead I saw a slice of cake that "needed eating up" and so I put that on my plate instead. Turns out it should have been enjoyed yesterday but I dutifully ate it up anyway (because we do not waste food!) but my need to have something lovely still had not been met. Though my calorie intake was satisfied, my NEED was not. So I ate the aforementioned peanut butter cookies as well. And now I feel a little poorly.

What does this have to do with Third Culture Kids? The stories I tell in this mundane little scenario have everything to do with my history. Many grow up with an anti-waste policy but my story also weaves an intimate relationship with famine into this message. My religious upbringing lent me a certain ambivalence around "indulgence" too – hence my easy disregard of what I actually wanted in the first place.

In other words, I told myself a story of "shouldn't waste" which combined with de-prioritising my actual felt need for loveliness, meaning I got the worst of all worlds. The danger of this is that my slight queasiness could easily encourage a narrative that sugar is bad and that I deserve what I got. A hard story, a story that tells us we shouldn't do this or that, and that if we do we will be less worthy of love.

So many of us carry hard stories. Stories that tell us:

"You have to keep people happy so they will love you."

"You have to be thinner so people will love you."

"If I make all the right decisions, I will be worthy."

"If I work till exhaustion, I'll know I've worked hard enough."

We tend to carry these stories as grown-ups trying to figure out the rules, whilst carrying anxiety about not being able to do it "right". Does this sound familiar? As TCKs we are constantly trying to figure out the (new) majority culture, find our way into it, and persuade others that we belong and are worthy of inclusion. And that inclusion often feels conditional.

In other words, I *did* do exactly what I wanted to do. I wanted to feel like a good person. Why? Because people like good people. And other people (majority cultures) get to determine the qualifying features of a "good person." And my internal story, the one I'm running on a loop, says that to be a good person I should eat the thing that will create least waste. And drink all the coffee you made while it's hot, even if you aren't enjoying it anymore.

My need to be a good person will always, always outweigh other needs – these other needs are less critical to my sense of social safety after all. So when I feel I am compulsively doing something I don't really want to do, or holding back from doing something I do want to do, it is worth pausing the self-criticism and frustration a moment to get curious and ask, "What is it about this that is making me feel like a better person than if I don't do it this way?"

In many ways, it is useful to be able to adapt this way. It aids social involvement and helps create a sense of safety that we feel control over – like an algorithm we can work out. How to be accepted: if I do (a) they'll do (b). Or if I do (c) they'll think I'm (d).

Ultimately this is how human beings work – we will sacrifice a lot to our need to feel like a good person. I hope my silliness about cookies doesn't distract from the power that this has over so many daily moments. Whether I impose my opinion in a conversation or not will be heavily linked to whether I believe it will make me a better or worse person for doing so. Whether I say yes to this relationship or no to that career opportunity is very much influenced by my belief in these stories I have created about myself – stories which are themselves influenced by those I was taught in the cultures where I was raised.

This brings us to the crux of the complication: different cultures have different sets of "good people" expectations. We can easily feel paralysed by the horrible reality that achieving good person status in one cultural context may be precisely what gets us ostracised in another cultural context. So, how do we decide on a story to live by?

Sifting through the stories we've accumulated and deciding which ones best serve the story we want to write in the future is a lot of work. Sometimes we worry that even this process of sifting is dismissive or critical of the stories we have lived so far. Or that it is critical of the people who taught us how to be "good" in these contexts. And yet, we can assess how helpful our past stories have been to us without forgetting how important these chapters have been to our lives. Choosing our story moving forward is not rejecting the story that has been – instead, we simply recognise that for our current context, past adaptations are no longer helpful.

So, if we are allowed to choose the story that serves us best, what would mine sound like today? "I'm worthy when I eat more than I want to *and* when I eat just what I want to. But turns out my body is happier when I listen to its needs." Next time, I'll just eat the cookies.

Does Travel Make me a Better Person?

A lot of us travel because we like the stimulation it brings to our lives. It connects us to parts of our story. But sometimes I encounter the belief that travel is itself a virtue. The thinking goes something like:

"My experiences of travel are what make me interesting. Ergo, should I stop travelling I would become mundane, boring."

While it is widely accepted that global engagement through travel develops many positive characteristics – such as increased cultural awareness – we do need to be wary of the broader implications of the sentiment. It is all too easy to imply, to others and to ourselves, that those who travel are made tolerant and open by their experiences and that the less travelled must necessarily lack these same characteristics.

I enjoy the article "Five Reasons Travel Does Not Make You a Better Person."[1] It is an entertaining read, but also does a great job of challenging some of the glibber assumptions we can make about the impact of travel. I especially love this perceptive observation:

"It's the vagueness of it that is so peculiar – not "I want to go to Colombia to see the incredible variety of bird species", or "I've always been fascinated by Russian architecture and I'd like to see it for myself", just a generalised desire to be somewhere else."

Now, doesn't that sound familiar? Beyond this, the article notes that this vagueness around the assumptions we hold around travel – namely that it makes us better people – serves to entrench barriers between the well-travelled and the less-well-travelled, and between those who want to travel more and those who are content to stay near "home."

The vast majority of my clients come to me desiring community. After all, many TCKs were raised in close-knit communities of expats, in international schools of similar "Others", and these communities are what we often most closely identify as "home". One of the biggest hurdles we face as we work through how to nurture and invest in our own communities as adults is our own "terminal uniqueness."[2]

If, in our more honest moments, we can acknowledge some of the beliefs that make travel a moral imperative, we can perhaps begin to notice how this obstructs our community building efforts through complex filtering mechanisms that keep the less travelled at bay. Perhaps we even tell ourselves it's not worth investing locally at all, because we will soon leave. After all, that's just who we are – we can't be tied down by the mundane. With Disney's Belle we cry, "There must be more than this provincial life!"

How about a radical alternative? You are interesting. Full stop. And so are they.

What if we could harness our "interesting" experiences to connect with the equally interesting experiences of others? Can our uniqueness be harnessed through the power of empathy and imagination to connect with others, and so end our loneliness?

You cannot fail at your identity. You cannot be less of a TCK, MK, Military Brat, business kid or cosmopolitan because you have stopped travelling, be it a pause or an indefinite stilling.

We can move past the terror of stillness, of settling, and find peace in Selves that can connect with Others here and now. We can do community. We have done global. We can do local, too. Travel does not get to have all the fun.

Travel does not make you a better person. You are intrinsically wonderful.

---

[1] Hanks, O. (2016). FIVE REASONS WHY TRAVEL DOESN'T MAKE YOU A BETTER PERSON. [online] *The Norwich Radical*. Available at: https://thenorwichradical.com/2016/04/08/five-reasons-why-travel-doesnt-make-you-a-better-person/ [Accessed 21 Nov. 2022].

[2] Bennett, J., 1993. Cultural Marginality: Identity Issues in Intercultural Training. In Paige, E. M., ed., 1993. *Education for the Intercultural Experience.* Intercultural Press: Yarmouth, Maine. pp. 109-136

Self-Compassion
and the Third
Culture Kid

I marvel at how often self-compassion (or the lack of it!) comes up in my work with Third Culture Kids. I shouldn't be surprised. After all, my own therapists point it out in me, too. But it does seem a strange kind of paradox that TCKs, who we all talk about as tending towards high levels of empathy and compassion towards *others* struggle so much in *self* compassion.[1,2]

What is compassion, anyway?

I'll spare you the dictionary definition approach and instead explain what I mean when I use this. To my mind, compassion accompanies empathy. It is the care and concern we feel for someone. Compassion is born of both observation and the ability to imagine the experience of another. It suspends judgement about whether or not this experience is "right" or "reasonable" and instead simply cares about it. Just as empathy is a necessary precursor to compassion (we need to be able to imagine the experience of another to activate care for that experience), compassion itself often leads us on to compassionate actions or responses to what we are observing. When feeling compassion, we feel the urge to ease burden, to communicate love. In other words, compassion propels us towards connection. We can't stay aloof or distant, for we care too much. Compassion gets us invested, not just in the present situation but in the feelings of those involved.

What is compassion good for?

The easy answer is that it is good for society. When people care about each other, they treat each other well. When we are invested in each other's feelings and experiences, we tend to work for each other's good. This increases cohesiveness in groups and raises trust and a general sense of security and interdependence.

Sounds great! Now, why do we need self-compassion?

Sometimes we don't feel that people care about us. We feel they don't understand us. That they aren't invested in us or what is good for our security or growth. That we can't count on them to really see us and know us. We feel disconnected and maybe even judged for our perspectives or behaviours.

Most of us have been here at some point in our lives, and Third Culture Kids especially so. In these circumstances it is easy to conclude one of two things:

People are awful and not worth bothering with. I don't need them anyway.

I am unlovable. No one will ever understand me because I am wired wrong. I am a defective human. I must be or they would want to know me.

The first response is born of lack of compassion: not having enough given to us, we decide we cannot afford to give anything.

The second response is born of lack of compassion, too: not having enough given to us, we decide this is because we don't deserve it.

Both are cripplingly painful experiences. Self-compassion stands in the gap.

In the first instance, self-compassion offers to ourselves what we need so that we aren't operating from deficit. We can continue to offer compassion to the world, because we have offered it to ourselves first. We can stay connected to the world, because we are connected to ourselves.

In the second instance, self-compassion reminds us how it feels to be understood and cared for, keeping us connected enough to that experience that when others do offer it to us, we recognise it and can accept it.

So, what does self-compassion look like?

It looks like compassion. Toward ourselves. It does just what compassion toward others does but directed inward.

Self-compassion observes what we are experiencing: "I'm feeling just awful".

We suspend judgement about whether we "should" be feeling awful. We activate care instead: care for the person we are, who is feeling awful.

Here self-compassion propels us to help ourselves feel better. We consider what happened that led us to feel awful and how understandable it is that we do, given what we know about ourselves and our story (self-knowing without judgement). We explore if there is anything we need in order to feel better – is there a misunderstanding we want to clarify? Is there a hot drink and a bit of self-care that could soothe us in the moment?

Self-compassion does not change our situations – though we often see the compassionate actions that can come next to do just this. Self-compassion itself simply pays attention. To us. To our needs. To our feelings. That attention is a kind of magic.

Self-compassion changes nothing about our situation – but it changes everything about how we *feel* about ourselves in our situation.

Self-compassion offers us an ally. We become our own friend.

And we all know the difference a friend can make.

---

[1] Mobbs, C. H. (2016) Benefits and challenges of TCK life. [online] *Expat Child*. Available at: https://expatchild.com/benefits-challenges-tck/.

[2] Pogosayan, M. (2016) Finding Home Between Worlds. [online] *Psychology Today*. Available at: https://www.psychologytoday.com/us/blog/between-cultures/201603/finding-home-between-worlds.

Essaying Identity

Identities are constructed from birth, delicately built upon the foundations our families set down for us, letting us know who we are through reciprocal mirroring. Positive and negative reactions to our Selves gradually solidify for us a sense of who we feel we are, and who other people think we are. If we are fortunate, there is some consensus between the two.

Peers are incredibly important in this mirroring as we grow up, and our field of reference expands from our immediate family to the cultural worlds that surround us. James describes a child's peers as instrumental in the development of their identity, writing that "identities emerge slowly, to be tried and tested out in the company, largely, of other children."[1] In other words, we grow up "essaying" identity. We try different versions out, like clothes, to see what fits us well, what makes us feel good, what seems to be preferred by others too. Gradually, we build up a wardrobe. And in doing so, we build a sense of what kind of person we are, that enjoys these particular clothes.

For Third Culture Kids, expatriate kids, or others from highly transitory backgrounds, the instability of these peer groups can make it hard for a consistent sense of self to "stick". As adults, our chameleon identities can be both blessing and challenge, as we navigate the cultural worlds around us, continued travel, and/or experiments in settledness. Our wardrobe keeps changing, as both our environment and our audience does too.

So many of us feel ourselves to be a different self in different places. As our peer groups differ from place to place, so do our selves, as we adapt and respond to different cultural surroundings. Language always plays a significant part here: in one country I am fluent, and vivacious wit abounds. In another, my speech is halting, and my Self responds to my peers with more hesitance: I am a more withdrawn or 'shy' version of myself. In America, my worldview may appear on a different end of the political spectrum than it does in the United Kingdom or Australia. My faith may have different expression, my sense of humour be more or less mainstream, or "appropriate".

Essaying identity becomes more risky with this kind of change. We might start to find ourselves reducing down to a capsule wardrobe, trying on only those clothes that seem to be universally approved of or useful.

Moreover, leaving a place is also often inextricably linked to the leaving of an identity role or status, or the taking on of a new one. Perhaps a career has ended, or a job role is changing. Perhaps you are leaving an old relationship behind or moving nearer to a new one. Perhaps you are leaving a community in which you were a leader, for one that does not yet recognise you as a valuable member. Perhaps you are leaving a place in which you were an outsider for one that holds the potential of reinvention and the hope of belonging.

Different identities hold different levels of usefulness in different contexts. And we, in our developmental years, notice. We may costume change multiple times a day with alacrity, whizzing through identities quickly to find the one most "appropriate" here. Or we may find ourselves paralysed, feeling stuck in the one outfit – too hot or too cold – simply because we don't seem to be able to shuffle the data quickly enough to understand where we are supposed to fit here.

Recognising the many selves that form throughout the places through which we pass is an important step towards settledness of Self. Settledness need not mean geographical stability, though for some this is a desirable element, but settledness of Self holds tight to the notion that we can nurture a core sense of Self that bends with change but does not break.

A core Self can be nurtured from our different cultural selves, so that our multiple expressions of self do not need to threaten our sense of integrity or authenticity. Instead this deeper sense of self can flex to give full expression to the complete complexity of our identity.

When we feel confident in who we are, in all the selves we hold having intrinsic value, then we can begin to essay identity again. We can trust in the kaleidoscope of self to steady, holding shape to reflect our story as makes most sense to us, with both clarity and compassion.

---

[1] James, A. (1993). *Childhood identities*. Edinburgh University Press.

The adult Third
Culture Kid parent:
when history does
NOT repeat

Writing about the Third Culture Kid parent is a big topic, and one that's hard to get right. When I examine myself, however, the reason I avoid it is that it feels vulnerable.

There is nothing like becoming a parent to make us realise that we really are making this up as we go along. Sure, there are books and courses and theories and approaches – and they all help construct a kind of framework to which we cling. But when our children are struggling in friendships, or we are struggling with their routine hysteria about flies and bees, we realise the books have not met our child.

What's more, Third Culture Kid parents have not lived the lives of their children. Now, this is the case for any parent, right? The world is always a different place for our children than it was for us. As my own child informs me when I suggest she find something to do without a screen, "It was okay for you, Mummy – you were *used* to being bored. You didn't have screens like I do."

Yet the general trajectory for parenting throughout the ages is that we learn from the model of our own experiences of being parented. We keep elements of that experience we appreciated (even if only with hindsight!) and we discard or replace those elements that we consciously did not enjoy. Many of us (dare I say most?) nevertheless find ourselves perpetuating the models we experienced, despite conscious attempts to deviate. The brain has learnt how parenting "should" look and we easily replicate it.

Fundamentally, there are two kinds of TCK parent: those raising TCKs and those raising non-TCKs.

The adult Third Culture Kid parent raising TCKs has both advantages and disadvantages to their experience. They have a "heads up" about the experiences of their TCK children and are better equipped to communicate understanding and empathy to them. But they also have the challenge of consciously noticing that despite the TCK connection, their children will have a different TCK experience from their own. And, if memories of my own teenage years serve me well, no child wants to be understood *too* well. We don't want to feel ourselves collapsing into our parents' identities and stories. We are trying to carve our own – leaving our own unique set of fingerprints all over its pages. We want our parents to recognise ideas and concepts in our stories, but rather than leave us with a sense of having only second-hand chapters to repeat, we want them to help us name our experiences more clearly.

The adult TCK raising TCKs gets to support their children in unique ways, sharing a unique set of experiences with them. Yet we must remember that our children's stories are themselves unique.

Then there is the second category of TCK parent: the adult Third Culture Kid raising non-TCKs. My sense is that the experiences of this group are less discussed. We tend to focus more on how parents in general can support their TCK children and I wonder how much it is because our tendency is to focus on the special needs of the TCK child; a non-TCK child's childhood must be so much more straightforward, right? In many ways, yes – I think it is. But it doesn't follow that it is more straightforward for an adult TCK to parent a non-TCK child. After all, it is this kind of childhood that is less known to us.

This non-TCK childhood is full of play dates with children – that stay. It involves friendship conflicts that have time to resolve, evolve, and transform slowly over time. This childhood has place/space-based traditions that can feel like they take on a life of their own. This childhood might involve less social, racial, or linguistic diversity than some of us would consider ideal. This childhood involves a child that is perhaps much more impacted by the constant presence of their peer group than we ever were.

We relive our own childhoods when we become parents. It is common for us to revisit difficult memories and experiences especially when our children hit the same age or developmental milestones we were at when traumatic events occurred to us. But non-TCK children are living such a different life that our very unfamiliarity of their experience can trigger a sense of incompetence or fear of "getting it wrong" that is already so prevalent for many of us.

I only spent two years of my primary school education in England, and those two years were not consecutive. My daughter now has

7 years (plus pre-school) under her belt. I spent my years confused and disorientated, with a minimal sense of friendship. My daughter, though occasionally preoccupied with the waxing and waning of her friendships, has an understanding of her social life that is unfamiliar to me. How do I navigate her through waters I have not sailed through myself? It is a peculiar challenge.

Some of us gravitate toward this challenge. After all, it is simply another culture to learn, and we have our own little guides to learn from. For others, this might feel like one unknown culture too many. Our little guide needs more of our leadership than we feel able to offer and the disorientation is real.

Parenting as an adult TCK is not without complication. And we are complicated people. And who knew how complicated our little ones were going to be either?!

Understanding leads to compassion. Compassion leads to nurture. Nurture walks us into growth. And then, as our children grow, we grow too.

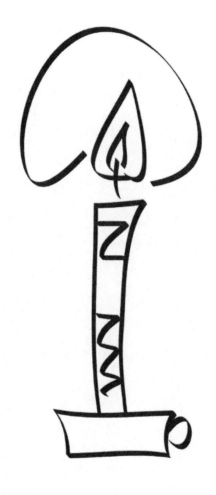

Third Culture Kids
and Burnout

I had been dragging for a few days. Everything was fine – great even – and I am REALLY good at noticing when things aren't okay. I am *so* great at noticing when things aren't okay that I sometimes take a big stick and poke "just fine" into a big pile of "not okay", just so I can say, "I found the next thing to work on!"

Yep. I'm a Third Culture Kid who sometimes finds it hard to cope when things are fine for too long.

I am wired for change, growth, and adaptation. Finding myself queen of the life I have been doggedly constructing for years, finding that life can adapt around *me* – now, *that* is scary stuff.

Not "eek!" scary. But the scary of seeing your reflection in a funhouse mirror that turns your image upside down, or so wavy that your silhouette is barely recognisable. It's you, but in a form that is strange to your own eyes.

Like many of us wired for the BIG changes, "samey fineness" can feel a little triggering for me – either because it is not emotionally stimulating enough, or because it feels like the calm before an inevitable storm. We feel the residual strain of the "waiting to move" element of our journey – a case of "any moment now…" when the bottom drops out of our daily routine and relationships.

I have noticed this restlessness turns up for me fairly regularly. I have learnt to recognise when it is a constructive prompt to address a stagnating area of my life, and when I am prodding my stick at something that really doesn't need the bruising.

But this restlessness was more tired. More discontented with self. More anxious. These felt like signs of burnout.

Psychology Today gives a good overview of what burnout means, and what it's about.[1] While I didn't feel the compassion fatigue many authors on the topic refer to, I was feeling the lethargy associated with burnout. This phrase especially caught me:

"The cynicism, depression, and lethargy that are characteristic of burnout most often occur when a person is not in control of how a job is carried out, at work or at home, or is asked to complete tasks that conflict with their sense of self."[1]

And then I remembered to count the years I had spent in this house – they numbered eight at the time of writing. Five years was my personal best, and then we were at eight. Many TCKs have a certain rhythm they are raised with. It might be two-year postings, a move every summer, or (like for me) three to four years in the host country, one year in the passport country. Eight years here means I am coming to the end of my second posting to this "country" as my internal clock would see it. The fact that autumn is upon us, and I first moved here in November is not lost on me either.

To approach the end of a posting is to feel a certain disengagement, a loss of control over one's daily routine. You are surrounded by boxes, goodbyes, and the ending of things. For many of us, a sense of "what's the point?" crept in as we considered spending the time we had left with people. What could be the purpose of that? We couldn't take them with us, and we may even have felt we no longer served any purpose in their lives.

Burnout for the TCK might well look like this: a sense of "what's my point?" creeping into every moment of the day.

In my case? Everything was fine, but I was feeling increasingly pointless and purposeless.

And then I read this:

"To counter burnout, having a sense of purpose, having an impact on others, or feeling as if one is making the world a better place are all valuable."[1]

Of course. Purpose is a topic that comes up so much in my work with Third Culture Kids. We seek a way of feeling we are making a difference in the world around us, and this is so often complicated by being raised in families or organisations with a clear sense of globally focused purpose. Finding our own sense of purpose is complicated by comparison with this kind of purpose-of-origin, and by the rhythm of our own mobility.

How can we achieve our purpose when our time in place to do so is often truncated, severed, interrupted?

How can we identify our purpose when our meaning to the people and culture around us changed so often?

We set our own purpose.

This is no mean feat in a world that has names for us depending on our different roles in society – mother, sister, husband, employee, etc. These names carry expectations with them, ways we can "correctly" fulfil the roles we have taken. But what if we could focus on our own expectations of ourselves within these roles? That would bring our wibbly wobbly funhouse mirror reflection into clarity.

"What is the purpose of my different identities?" I asked myself. The question itself is grounding. I am assuming I have purpose. By assuming purpose, I can stay engaged in my geographical and physical world because now I am in control of my mobility rhythms. I don't need to disengage from my purpose in preparation for the lack of control that is coming, or the sense that tasks I am facing are ill-matched to my identity.

I am in control. I choose my tasks. I define my purpose.

And so, while I still get tired and I still have to be mindful of self-care and of rest, I can avoid burnout by reminding myself of my purpose.

My purpose in my relationships.

My purpose in my community.

My purpose as a therapist.

My purpose as housekeeper of my home.

Even my purpose as a pet owner!

I can define these roles and resource myself to meet them to the best of my ability and to my own satisfaction. No need to burn out when we are queen (or king!) of our own lives.

No need to burn. Instead, we shine.

---

[1] Psychology Today (2019). Burnout. [online] *Psychology Today*. Available at: https://www.psychologytoday.com/us/basics/burnout.

Joy in the Normal

All my life I have struggled with the word "normal".

The word was virtually taboo in the expatriate community I grew up in, being seen to be synonymous with ordinary, boring, and mundane. As expat children growing up "among worlds" we knew we were special, had special experiences, had special outlooks.[1] Visits to our "home" countries would be punctuated with comments from family, friends and 'home' communities identifying us as mature, with widened horizons, and wiser than our years. Indeed, the idea is neatly summed up by Sheard when likening Third Culture Kids (expat kids) to "gifted children" – not a comparison I find especially helpful, but one that expresses quite well the identity attributed to many expat children.[2]

This outlook can be a useful one growing up; it explains the challenges of relating to different peer groups in different cultures in a way that counters the shame of alienation and renders unimportant the discomfort experienced in the numerous *faux pas* we make. After all, if we are special it's okay to feel different. If we feel like misfits, that's okay, we have a wonderful world view that compensates for not feeling "normal".

For many of us, not fitting in at home is a small price to pay for the experiences of our childhoods: the travel, the safaris, the bustling world of the expat, the educational opportunities, as well as the cultural jigsaw puzzles we learn to navigate with delight.

And yet many of us, at some point, often at the point of entering university or college, perhaps later as we start careers and grow families, take on new responsibilities that reduce our opportunities for adventure and we begin to mirror the community around us. Then an uncomfortable question rears its head: "Are we becoming normal?"

Throughout my research I encountered Third Culture Kids who expressed discomfort as they realised that, over time, they were increasingly resembling the communities in which they had become embedded. Many actively sought ways to continue to express their internally felt differences to those around them. Some TCKs get jobs that allow for more international interaction, others avoid pop culture, or orient themselves more globally. Others simply struggle in their increasing sense of invisibility and sense of perpetual uniqueness.

Feeling the extraordinary disappear and the normal creep in is hugely uncomfortable for those accustomed to living in the margins. It is a challenge that can be met in a couple of different ways, sometimes in combination if you are feeling especially creative!

First, as mentioned, we can find new outlets for our internally experienced differences. We can find ways to subtly but significantly distinguish ourselves to maintain our sense of self as "special". This need not be a case of indifference to those around us, nor expressive of a sense of superiority, but rather a thoughtful response to a deeply rooted need to maintain an early identity as special and unique. One interview respondent told me of her tendency to favour American over British writers when studying English Literature at a UK university. This bucked the curriculum's trend and offered her an opportunity to become knowledgeable in a niche area amongst her peer group. It did not scream "I'm special!" from the rooftops, but at this time in her life it supported an important part of her Self by setting herself apart in a small but significant way.

Secondly, we can practise finding joy in the mundane. This, I think, can be more of a challenge. We can choose not to despise the ordinary, or even being identified as members of the normal, and instead find joy in the average and the ordinary. When taken for a local we can feel flattered rather than alarmed, and can seek ways to get involved in our local communities. We can take joy in increased understanding of local politics and local concerns. After all, are these not signs of a new skill set gained, that of belonging?

What if, heresy of heresies, "normal" is the real adventure for TCKs?

---

[1] Pollock, D.C. and Van, R.E. (2009). *Third culture kids : growing up among worlds*. Boston: Nicholas Brealey Pub.

[2] Sheard, W. (2008). Lessons From Our Kissing Cousins: Third Culture Kids and Gifted Children. *Roeper Review*, 30(1), pp.31–38. doi:10.1080/02783190701836437.

Has your story been heard?

If a tree falls in the forest, but there is no one to hear it fall, does it make a sound?

Our stories need to be heard to feel real. For us to feel real. For the less "geographically challenged", the people they grow up with and spend years around become witnesses to their lives. Their shared experiences reach across all the senses to act as proofs to the stories that make up their lives.

For the TCK, however, witnesses disperse across the globe. Few, if any, in our current location could speak with authority about our history, having not been eyewitnesses themselves. Perhaps they do not even possess a second-hand account, our own mouths stoppered with a hesitation to share too much of our precious stories for fear of revealing ourselves as the aliens we are.

Our stories are real. They are our Truths, and we are the authority on them. But often the significance of our experiences has been blurred, put out of focus, by a lack of shared perspective with those around us. For many, including TCKs, even close family members have vastly different accounts and experiences of childhood memories and cultural identities. All this can contribute to a sense of un-reality, a blurriness about our Selves, a lack of confidence in our own Story.

For our stories to feel real, they must become tangible. How can our histories be experienced in the now, carried into the future, and shared with new witnesses, if they remain invisible and intangible? We need tangible objects that can represent our histories and our Selves, especially when walking, talking witnesses to our lives are lacking. These objects are the "identity props" I have discussed before.

Engage your senses – Sight, Sound, Touch, Taste and Smell – to bring your history to life through identity props. What pictures, artwork, jewellery, music, furniture, fabric, food, or perfumes can you collect – either in one place, or perhaps dispersed around your home? These are objects that represent parts of you, your story, and can bolster your belief and faith in your own experiences.

For me? When I'm feeling in need of comfort, or soul food, I dig out recipes of my favourite foods from West Africa and replicate them as best as I can. I have music that reminds me of home, and wax print fabrics that offer pleasing dissonance in my otherwise rather English home.

Remember, though, that your identity props will change and adapt over time. Your need for them will flex and alter. When I first moved into my home, I mounted some leather work pictures from my host country on the wall in pride of place. If pressed, I would have admitted I didn't really love them aesthetically, but they were powerfully representational to me regarding my story, and they witnessed to that story every time I had someone over for coffee.

Later, I took them down and replaced them with photographs of the people in my life now: the family and community that shape it and are acting as witnesses to my experiences now. This is not a case of my history disappearing, or even reducing in significance, but an instance of new witnesses emerging.

Your Story is Real. You are Real. Engage your senses to remind yourself of this today.

Third Culture Kids: Commitment in Relationship

I've been reading Lijadi and Schalkwyk's article, "Narratives of Third Culture Kids: Commitment and Reticence in Social Relationships."[1] It presents interesting insights around mobility addiction and adaptation versus commitment, where the Third Culture Kid experiences commitment less as conscious choice and more as "an imperative of merely accepting differences and learning to live with it."[1] One quotation from a Third Culture Kid especially caught my attention:

"I find that I am much more insecure with myself when I am with someone."[1]

The authors note that relationships for Third Culture Kids can present "a double-edged sword of simultaneously striving for independence and being dependent on the other."[1]

For many non-TCKs, relationships are developed over time with commitment motivated by choice rather than survival. For many TCKs, choice in committed relationships is a new and alarming prospect. The current literature describes our "cut and run" patterns, where often we will sever commitments and leave before we can be left. Personally, I have also noted the converse, where TCKs stay and remain unwitting martyrs to damaging relationships, thus playing out their "commit to survive" childhood patterns even into adulthood. Voluntary disengagement (even in pursuit of a healthier, happier life) can be a frightening prospect to someone who has had separation and disruption imposed on their lives from childhood.

Where am I going with this? How did we go from feeling more insecure when in relationship than when single to commitment-phobes and commitment-martyrs? I would suggest that both commitment responses are fear responses: they are protective mechanisms born out of insecurity. So why would Third Culture Kids feel more insecure when in relationship than when single? It is an interesting notion, especially when we consider the dominant narrative around people in relationship feeling more confident because they feel themselves to be attractive, accepted, and wanted. Long term relationship is what makes us feel safe, stable, and that we have found belonging, surely?

Perhaps not. Perhaps high mobility rewires us for independence to such an extent that the interdependence that inevitably grows in long-term relationships (and perhaps we should also include long-term friendships here) challenges our notions of the Self as independent. We leave our safe havens of independence to enter the murky world of dependence, which can unsurprisingly leave us feeling more insecure.

While we TCKs are typically good at connecting, engaging with people, and building relationship, the level and extent of commitment in these relationships is in question here. For many years I presumed my absence mattered not a great deal to my friends. This was not an issue of poor self-esteem, merely a reflection of the fact that I did not conflate friendship and reliance. Just because I liked someone did not mean that I felt a need for their presence, and I assumed the same was true vice-versa. Lijadi and Schalkwyk suggest that while Third Culture Kids are gifted connectors, they are reticent around commitment in their relationships. Commitment suggests responsibility, and a certain mutuality.

Pico Iyer wrote in *The Global Soul* about "a lack of accountability" that offers the Third Culture Kid another kind of double-edged sword: our independence offers us both freedom and exile.[2]

So many of the TCKs I work with are wrestling with the tension between relational independence and commitment. The former brings both a sense of safety and loneliness. The second brings a certain terror along with its hope for ongoing connection and belonging. It is important to recognise the validity of each approach to relationship, for each fulfils a different and completely valid need. It is also worth noting that the terror of commitment hints at many underlying beliefs we may be carrying that no longer serve us.

---

[1] Lijadi, A. and van Schalkwyk, G. (2014). Narratives of Third Culture Kids: Commitment and Reticence in Social Relationships. *The Qualitative Report*, 19(25). doi:10.46743/2160-3715/2014.1213.

[2] Iyer, P. (2000). *The global soul : jet lag, shopping malls, and the search for home.* New York: Knopf.

Balance: tightrope walkers, swings, and elephants

Balance. It has been a buzzword for a while, but especially comes into its own around January. The core of so many of our resolutions aim to bring life "back into balance" in some way. How has this year gone for you? Are you feeling more balanced? Or are you still feeling wobbly, precarious, about to topple? For Third Culture Kids, and any others who have lived through multiple transitions, balancing all the varying expectations and demands of life can feel like a game with perilously high stakes.

I believe there are three elements of life that work together to keep us in, or out, of balance. These are Belonging, Identity, and Place.

We experience identity as those attributed (nationality, race, ethnicity, age) and experienced (values, preferences, giftings, beliefs about self and others) – characteristics that we become known by, to others and to ourselves. Our identities might find expression through national affiliation, career or calling, a sense of our own uniqueness. Those expressions that affirm our stories and continue to develop and nurture our distinct contribution to the world around us – that's identity.

Belonging is what happens when our identities make sense to those around us. Belonging is what happens when we feel welcome alongside others with similar threads of identity to ourselves. Belonging can be found in family, friendships, romantic relationships, work environments, or more broadly in cultures and subcultures, such as music, literary, and artistic communities. Connections with others that affirm who we are, and where we are welcome – that's belonging.

We experience place as the vital and necessary context of our stories. Place explains where we became ourselves and provides the landscape in which we connect to others. We may be rooted in place, deeply connected to the immediate locality, or we may (as do many TCKs) exist slightly above the surface of our place(s), playing a perpetual game of 'floor is lava' with our lives, rather than the sofa cushions of our childhood.

When we feel ourselves to be out of balance, it can be a helpful exercise to ask ourselves which of the three elements is wobbling.

Is Place missing from our triad? Are we a tightrope walker floating above the earth, disconnected from our immediate environment? Or are we lacking context in some other way, with the places of our past so disconnected and distant that our own story feels out of focus?

Or is it our Identity that feels wobbly? Are we a swing, coming into existence only when others acknowledge or recognise us? Have we got competing Selves that refuse to cooperate, jostling each other out of definition? Lacking expression of Self, we seem to exist simply to become whatever those around us need or want us to be, becoming a vehicle for their stories and purposes rather than our own. We are grounded in Place, we are connected to others, but we are so obligingly adaptable to their purposes that our own identity and agenda feels ill-defined by comparison.

Or is it Belonging that is toppling us? Like the elephant on the circus ball, your disconnectedness feels conspicuous, perhaps even mildly ridiculous. There is so much of you, of your story – how can you possibly connect effectively with others? It feels as though there is nothing to grasp at to steady yourself. You know who you are, and where you are; your wobbles are rooted in your distinctiveness, your you-ness that seems to keep you apart, precarious and vulnerable.

Whichever you may feel yourself to be – tightrope walker, swing, or elephant on a ball – you are not alone! We all get out of balance at times. Perhaps we've never felt in balance. Here is the method behind the madness of my metaphors: when we can identify the area that wobbles, we can take steps to strengthen it. Knowledge really is power, and spending some dedicated time to explore ways of shoring up our sense of Place, our Identity, or our Belonging is time well spent.

Balance can be practised. Balance is within reach.

A thank you –
from me to you

It is not uncommon for a therapist to be on the receiving end of gratitude expressed by their clients. Noticing our own journey can prompt many feelings – frustration, pain, sadness, compassion, hope, pride – and gratitude to those who have journeyed with us along the way. I have been really moved by some of the expressions of thanks I have received over the last few years yet feel consistently inadequate in my own response.

You see, I am grateful to you. Whether we have worked together, or our only encounter thus far has been through this book, I am so grateful for the time you have taken to be here with me.

Thank you for taking the time to sit with your story as we have walked through these pages together.

Each chapter has been an invitation for you to listen to your own story more deeply. Many Third Culture Kids I work with have not told their full stories before. There can be shame or fear in the telling, but oh – there is also so much beauty. Your story is You. How you tell it is such a precious glimpse into the You that you carry through the world. By taking time to make space for your story, you encounter yourself in new ways. This deeper knowing of the self can only bring wonderful things to the world around you, as you give yourself more opportunities to share your story in new ways. And we need you – all of you – in this world today.

Thank you for your courage.

I hear so much pain every day. And so much fear. And so, so much courage. The courage it takes to click into a meeting with me, to show up, to invest in your own growth. In reading this book you have shown this courage too. It is immense, and I do not underestimate it. You are astonishing. The fire in your belly to grow is a continuous inspiration to me, and it warms my heart.

Thank you for prompting my tears.

Many Third Culture Kids discount their pain as not "enough" to warrant their tears. But as simple as it sounds, I maintain that sad things need tears. Tears are an honourable response to the presence of pain, and they bring congruence to our experiences by externalising our internal pain. Time and time again, writing to you has brought me to tears, and as I have watered my work with my tears, I am so grateful for the precious experience of knowing you. You and me, we are both worth tears – and I'm so thankful you have taken the time to read these thoughts of mine and reflect on the value of your story.

Thank you for the hope you kindle.

I am so grateful for the generosity of the Third Culture Kids I have met. I had this mad hope in 2015, when I founded Life Story Therapies, that compassionate understanding of their own stories would propel Third Culture Kids into the lives they wanted. The TCKs I have worked with caught that hope and kindled the embers. We nurse the fires together, in therapeutic alliance, mutual hope supporting growth. Hope comes to life in our sessions, and it is the most beautiful thing. In reading this collection of thoughts here I hope you have felt a similar stirring – a new or renewed self-compassion and gratitude for the energy you have brought to your story so far, the incredible you that you are, the courage it's taken to live this story of yours, and joyful hope in the story you have yet to write.

You have brightened my life, inspired me, and propelled me forward.

Thank you.

More of
Rachel's Story

Rachel Cason was born in Niger, growing up between the mission field and city life "at home" in England, with a year or so in France as a teenager. Consciously not-belonging to any of the cultural landscapes she moved between, sociology became a lifeline when she realised it could make sense of her experiences in liminal spaces. An early observer of group dynamics, she continued to apply these skills at Keele University where she achieved dual honours in sociology and French. A masters followed, and then a doctorate which allowed her to focus exclusively on the experiences of Third Culture Kids of all ages and backgrounds around identity, belonging and relationship to place. This research was the catalyst for Life Story Therapies, where Rachel works with TCKs using methodology born directly from her research experiences.

Rachel's current focus is on working with adult TCKs to honour their stories so far, and compassionately support any changes they want to make for their future chapters. When she's not working, she's writing her own story - whose particular adventure right now is focused on settledness. To date this looks like getting to grips with home improvements, building local connection, exploring local landscapes, delighting in family life, and figuring out her relationship with her cat! Settling in a small Lincolnshire town has been her biggest adventure so far, with many trips, stumbles and clumsy successes that continue to challenge and enrich her story.

Website:	**www.explorelifestory.com**
Email:	**rachelcason@explorelifestory.com**
Facebook:	**www.facebook.com/explorelifestory**
Instagram:	**www.instagram.com/rachel.cason.lifestory**
Podcast:	**shows.acast.com/explore-your-story**